W9-AHJ-461

INSIGHT ⊙ GUIDES

EXPLORE

ROME

PLAN & BOOK
YOUR TAILOR-MADE TRIP

BRAZIL **CHILE** **ECUADOR**

TAILOR-MADE TRIPS & UNIQUE EXPERIENCES CREATED BY LOCAL TRAVEL EXPERTS AT INSIGHTGUIDES.COM/HOLIDAYS

Insight Guides has been inspiring travellers with high-quality travel content for over 45 years. As well as our popular guidebooks, we now offer the opportunity to book tailor-made private trips completely personalised to your needs and interests.
By connecting with one of our local experts, you will directly benefit from their expertise and local know-how, helping you create memories that will last a lifetime.

HOW INSIGHTGUIDES.COM/HOLIDAYS WORKS

STEP 1

Pick your dream destination and submit an enquiry, or modify an existing itinerary if you prefer.

STEP 2

Fill in a short form, sharing details of your travel plans and preferences with a local expert.

STEP 3

Your local expert will create your personalised itinerary, which you can amend until you are completely satisfied.

STEP 4

Book securely online. Pack your bags and enjoy your holiday! Your local expert will be available to answer questions during your trip.

BENEFITS OF PLANNING & BOOKING AT
INSIGHTGUIDES.COM/HOLIDAYS

PLANNED BY LOCAL EXPERTS
The Insight Guides local experts are hand-picked, based on their experience in the travel industry and their impeccable standards of customer service.

SAVE TIME & MONEY
When a local expert plans your trip, you save time and money when you book, even during high season. You won't be charged for using a credit card either.

TAILOR-MADE TRIPS
Book with Insight Guides, and you will be in complete control of the planning process, from the initial selections to amending your final itinerary.

BOOK & TRAVEL STRESS-FREE
Enjoy stress-free travel when you use the Insight Guides secure online booking platform. All bookings come with a money-back guarantee.

WHAT OTHER TRAVELLERS THINK ABOUT TRIPS BOOKED
AT INSIGHTGUIDES.COM/HOLIDAYS

Trip to Portugal

Every step of the planning process and the trip itself was effortless and exceptional. Our special interests, preferences and requests were accommodated resulting in a trip that exceeded our expectations.

Corinne, USA   ★★★★★

Trip to Vietnam

The organization was superb, the drivers professional, and accommodation quite comfortable. I was well taken care of! My thanks to your colleagues who helped make my trip to Vietnam such a great experience.

Heather   ★★★★★

CONTENTS

ART IN CHURCHES

Take in the spectacular mosaics of Santa Maria in Trastevere (route 10), the grand elegance of Santa Maria Maggiore (route 12), or the Renaissance masterpieces of Santa Maria del Popolo (route 7).

RECOMMENDED ROUTES FOR...

CHILDREN

Head for the Villa Borghese park (route 7), where the kids will love boating in the Giardino del Lago, as well as the puppet theatre and zoo. The Explora Children's Museum is lots of fun too (see page 23).

CLASSIC CAFÉS

Drink in Rome's literary history at Antico Caffè Greco (route 5). For spectacular views, try Casina Valadier in the Pincio Gardens (route 7). For people-watching, try one of Trastevere's many cafés (route 10).

FINE ART ENTHUSIASTS

An extraordinary collection of ancient art and statuary can be found at the Capitoline Museums (route 1). Leave plenty of time for the Vatican Museums, especially Michelangelo's ceiling at the Sistine Chapel (route 8).

FOOD AND WINE

The Jewish Ghetto (route 10) is where to find hearty Roman dishes. For a picnic try the market at Campo de' Fiori (route 3), or Volpetti, one of the city's best delis (route 11). The Castelli Romani are a foodie delight (route 16).

HISTORY BUFFS

Explore the heart of Ancient Rome (route 1) and the Colosseum (route 2), or head out further afield to the well-preserved ruins of Ostia Antica (route 17) and the ancient burial sites of the Appian Way (route 14).

ROMANTIC ROME

Stroll amid the orange trees of the Parco Savello (route 11), enjoy the view from the terrace of the Pincio Gardens (route 7), take a boat trip along the Tiber or head for Tivoli's Villa d'Este (route 15).

SHOPPING

Rome's most opulent shopping street is Via dei Condotti (route 5), while an interesting mix of chic boutiques and studios can be found in the neighbourhood of Monti (route 13).

INTRODUCTION

An introduction to Rome's geography, customs and culture, plus illuminating background information on cuisine, history and what to do when you're there.

Visiting the Colosseum

EXPLORE ROME

Few other places command the respect and awe of the visitor the way the city of Rome does. The multifaceted and layered nature of the modern city is as much a draw as the ancient monuments, Renaissance palaces, and grandeur of the Vatican.

Rome has long been called the Eternal City. It is difficult to tell if the name refers to the city as the seat of the Roman Empire, as the heart of the Catholic Church, as the capital city of Italy, or as a major pilgrim destination. The layer upon layer of history certainly has an eternal feeling, but it is the continuously unfolding drama of the city that is its biggest draw.

Walking through the *centro storico* (historic centre), one is struck by the sheer size and majesty of the buildings crammed into the narrow, winding streets. Romans somehow manage to live amid their history with a surprising degree of indifference while rushing about their daily lives, and this is something of the appeal of the city.

ARCHITECTURE

The disregard of the local population for their extraordinary surroundings has a natural explanation in overfamiliarity. Rome is a city standing on the shoulders of its predecessors: medieval churches rise from the remains of ancient houses; a Renaissance palace balances on top of the Theatre of Marcellus, standing next to 20th-century apartments. The shapes of streets and piazzas often echo the preceding architectural spaces, providing a sense of discovery at every turn. It's not just the monumental sights that take the eye, either: look out for that shady courtyard with a fountain, that flower growing between ancient marble ruins or a Baroque façade above a modern café.

Ancient and medieval Rome

Though the shape of the city has developed over three millennia, there were distinct phases of construction. Much of ancient Rome was built between the 1st century BC and 3rd century AD. Many of the buildings in the centre have ancient ruins in their foundations. These were added to in the late medieval period, when resources were limited.

With the return of the Papacy from Avignon in the 1370s, there was a renewed interest in construction and civic maintenance that lasted well into the Renaissance. After the restoration of several aqueducts, the addition of fountains and water features to public spaces became a Roman obsession.

The legendary Da Baffetto pizzeria

The Renaissance

A huge number of Rome's architectural gems date from the Renaissance (mid-15th to 17th century), when the city was again a cultural centre at the heart of Europe. This period saw major building of palaces, roads, piazzas and churches, as each noble family tried to outshine their neighbours. This was the age of the Baroque, perfected by Gianlorenzo Bernini – his theatrical and bold Rome is an open-air gallery of fountains, façades and curves.

Unified Italy

Grand boulevards and huge public works buildings were not added until the post-Unification era of the 1870s. Again the face of Rome was permanently changed with the addition of floodwalls on the banks of the Tiber, the expansion of neighbourhoods, and the destruction of ancient ruins and medieval quarters to build 'modern' monuments and straight streets in the new capital city. This idea was picked up again under the Fascist regime of Mussolini, who wanted not only grand architecture to represent his ideals but also architecture to represent industry.

The 20th century

Following World War II, vast neighbourhoods were rebuilt using cheap construction materials to provide inexpensive post-war housing. Sections of Rome damaged in Allied bombing raids were rebuilt, and restaurants and businesses were remodelled with the ubiquitous 1960s-era terrazzo floors, chrome and wood panelling.

The 21st century

In a city dominated by its monumental past and traditional values, some of the best-known modern architects are daring to make their mark. Genoese architect Renzo Piano's state-of-the-art Auditorium, opened in 2002, spawned a wave of ultramodern architectural projects.

These include Richard Meier's controversial pavilion housing the Ara Pacis (an ancient Roman altar), which, like it or loathe it, is a major new landmark on the cityscape. It's the first modern building to be constructed in the historic centre since Mussolini's Fascist era, and is a little too modern for some tastes. The vast sums spent on the project are difficult to justify, say its detractors, in a city with thousands of neglected archaeological remains.

There's also Zaha Hadid's ambitious contemporary art centre (National Museum of 21st-Century Arts, known as **MAXXI**), in the northern suburbs, completed in 2009, and **The Cloud**, Fuksas' convention centre, opened in 2016, and the **Centrale Montemartini museum**, an imaginatively converted electrical power plant in Ostiense housing part of the Capitoline Museums' vast collection of ancient statuary.

Deli owner Alessandro Volpetti

CITY LAYOUT

The face of the city is defined by its natural topography. Originally, Rome was founded on the famous Seven Hills that sit on the right bank of the snaking Tiber River. The hills of the Aventine, Capitoline, Caelian, Esquiline, Palatine, Quirinale, and Viminale and the valleys in between have been inhabited since at least 1000 BC. These areas still form the core of the city centre, but over the ages Rome has expanded to include the Pincio Hill to the north, and the Janiculum Hill (Gianicolo) across the river. The *centro storico* is a relatively small area defined by the 3rd-century Aurelian Wall. Compact and walkable, it extends across the river to include Trastevere.

20th-century developments

In the early-20th century, new construction following Unification added districts such as Prati, the Via Veneto, Castro Pretorio, Salario and pretty Parioli. A great influx of population post-World War II further expanded the city in a middle-class urban sprawl, extending south along the Via Ostiense, and north to the *grande raccordo anulare* (GRA or ring road). The satellite city of EUR, or *Esposizione Universale di Roma*, was built as a Fascist-era utopia in the 1930s. Construction was halted with the fall of Mussolini, and the area has now been inhabited by several generations of Romans.

Port city

In the heat of summer, Rome does not feel like it is on the water, yet in many ways it is a port town. The nearby Ostia sits at the mouth of the Tiber floodplain, along a stretch of perfect Mediterranean beach. Ostia Antica was the major port of ancient Rome, bringing supplies up the river from all parts of the world.

The riverside atmosphere was inseparable from life in Rome, and, up until around a century ago, inhabitants would hop in their skiff to fish or row across the Tiber. The city centre's watery feel changed dramatically with the construction of the floodwalls that now line its banks.

PEOPLE

Considering that Rome is the capital city of Italy it has a relatively low population. Around 2.9 million residents live in the city proper, with a total of 4.3 million in the greater metropolitan area. There is a general feeling of crowded sidewalks and noisy traffic, which is more indicative of the Italian culture than actual numbers of people.

Italy is a family-based society, but most young Romans are cosmopolitan enough to at least wish they could contradict the *mammoni* stereotype, which generally describes Italians as unwilling to leave their mamma's home until they get married. Shortage of jobs and the extremely high rents, however, make it

Italian chic   *Guard, Palazzo del Quirinale*

impossible for most Romans to leave their nest, and many just can't afford to say bye to mum until they are in their 40s, or even 50s.

After a rightwing intermezzo with Gianni Alemanno, in June 2013 the Eternal City confirmed its leftist tra-dition by electing mayor transplant surgeon Ignazio Marino. Marino pedestrianized Via die Fori Imperiali and fought unlicensed vending. He was forced to resign by his own party in October 2015. In 2016, Virginia Raggi, of the Five Star Movement,

---

DON'T LEAVE ROME WITHOUT...

Testing the waters. Some of the charm of Rome is the abundance of flowing water and decorative fountains. The early Romans built the great aqueduct system that supplied drinking water to the city. Fresh drinking water still runs freely for public consumption, and can be found in drinking fountains called *nasoni* (big noses).

Indulging in local superstitions. Do as Audrey Hepburn so famously did in *Roman Holiday*, and put your hand in the gaping Bocca della Verità, or 'Mouth of Truth', at the church of Santa Maria in Cosmedin. The story goes that fibbers will have their hands bitten off… Or throw a coin into the Trevi Fountain to ensure your return to the Eternal City. See page 38 and 53.

Eating for free. Head into one of the city's wine bars for pre-dinner drinks (usually from about 6pm) and you may find that there are nibbles laid on for free. This highly civilised Italian tradition is known as the aperitivo. See page 17.

Looking out for the local oranges. During the Roman Empire, exotic plants were imported from all over the world to deco-rate the city's gardens, and streets were planted with flower and fruit trees for a fes-tive look. To deter theft, a special orange was developed that produced fruit all year but was all completely inedible. The dec-orative sour orange is still grown in many public places in Rome. See page 76.

Indulging in some retail therapy. Svelte Romans saunter down Via del Corso and Via dei Condotti to win-dow-shop for designer names. More individualistic shopping awaits in the art galleries and workshops of Trastevere and the Borghetto Flaminio antiques market. See page 18.

Visiting a 'talking statue'. In Rome there are six 'talking statues', known as Il Congresso degli Arguti (the Congress of the Shrewd): Marforio, Facchino, Abate Luigi, Madama Lucrezia, Babu-ino and Pasquino. They formed a sort of anonymous political forum in 15th-cen-tury Rome, at a time when papal cen-sorship was strictly enforced. Criticism was originally directed towards political injustices and corruption in the Church, but eventually included lampooning. Pasquino is the only statue still in use. See page 42.

won nearly 66 percent of the vote and became the first woman to be elected mayor of Rome.

When in Rome

Rome has its own particular 'schedule', a pace that seems to defy all definitions of time management and practicality. This laissez-faire attitude often gives the impression that the Romans care little about the needs or time limitations of the visitor. The impression couldn't be further from the truth. Scratch below the surface of any Italian's seemingly indifferent façade and you will find a friend for life. The key to this lies in the immortal phrase, 'when in Rome do as the Romans'. Tourists and residents are simply expected to do what everyone else is doing. Insisting the local way isn't effective is generally met with a cold shoulder. If you ask Romans why, they will tell you, *è così*, that's the way it is.

Also important is making the right impression, as summed up by the phrase *fare una bella figura*. Translated literally as 'making a beautiful figure', this means 'to make a good impression'. This is not just an Italian idiom, but a fundamental life concept that governs beauty, image, aesthetic, behaviour and even entertainment. The belief ensures that conversation is appropriate, clothing is stylish, accessories match, facial expressions are gauged, and planned activities seem effortless. The choice of what to do, and with whom to do it, is often well considered.

CLIMATE

The classic Mediterranean climate is one of the main draws for visitors and immigrants alike. Rome has sunny weather for an average of 10 months a year. The winters can be cold and rainy, but temperatures rarely drop below 4°C (40°F). In contrast, summers are long and hot, with an average of 20°C (68°F) from mid-May through to mid-October, with temperatures in July and August well above the European average high of 28°C (83°F). April, May, September and October are usually the best months to visit.

A life outdoors

With the sunny warm days it is not surprising that life is lived outdoors. Restaurants are designed to spill out on the streets, windows are left wide open, and the workday is arranged so that people can enjoy a bit of sun at lunch. Romans are known for their stylish skimpy fashion, designed with heat in mind. They are also famous for their architectural styles, which make the best of the weather; balconies and rooftop terraces, shady courtyards and tree-lined piazzas.

Despite the eclectic look and chaos of the city centre it works surprisingly well. Romans know how to live the good life, and they do it outdoors. After you

View from the Pincio terrace, Villa Borghese

have had a chance to see the sights, wander the streets, and get your fill of museums and churches, find a café terrace or spot on a piazza and sit and watch the ebb and flow of this great city under the evening sky.

TOP TIPS FOR EXPLORING ROME

Appropriate dress. Modest clothing must be worn in the Basilica of St Peter's (and in all churches). This means no shorts, no sleeveless tops and no skirts above the knee. In the busy season vendors in the area sell a set of paper trousers, at inflated prices, for those caught without acceptable attire.

Papal audiences. These are held in the Vatican on Wednesday at 10.30am, except in the height of summer, when they are at the Pope's summer residence at Castel Gandolfo (see page 97) outside Rome. Apply for free tickets in writing to the Prefettura della Casa Pontificia, 00120 Città del Vaticano, or go to the office on the preceding Monday or Tuesday (it's through the bronze door watched over by Swiss Guards, to the right of the basilica). For more information, tel: 06-6988 3114. The Pope comes to a window above the piazza on Sunday at noon to give the traditional angelus blessing.

Summer on the island. Rome's river life can be enjoyed every summer from the city's own island, the Isola Tiberina. From June to September, it hosts a pleasant festival and is filled with restaurants, bars, market stands, and even an outdoor movie theatre.

River cruising. Rome's river life can be enjoyed from the water itself on a Tiber river cruise (Battelli di Roma). Boats depart from the southeast bank near the Ponte Sant'Angelo.

Bring your own. It's common practice throughout the Castelli to bring your own food to wine shops, pay for a glass or a carafe, and eat on the premises.

Tour on a shoestring. For the cheapest, most chaotic tour through Rome, hop on the 87 bus, which runs from east to west, scoring a cross-section of the city's history. It runs from bustling Piazza Cavour to the rural Via Appia Antica archaeological park. En route are swathes of the Imperial, early Christian, Renaissance and Baroque city in all its glory, from the Colosseum to Piazza Navona, the Tiber and the Seven Hills of Rome. To see Rome as Fellini saw it, ride the No. 3 tram, which Fellini claimed gave him inspiration.

Parking in Rome. If driving is a challenge, parking is an enigma. While you'll notice little regard for signage on the part of the locals, parking laws do exist. Your best bet is to look for blue painted lines and a large blue 'P'. You can pay by the hour with a machine and leave the receipt in the car. Parking lots (parcheggio) are also marked with a blue 'P' and are staffed by the hour and closed at night. Parcheggio Villa Borghese is the largest, most convenient, and most reliable. Entrance at 33 Viale del Galoppatoio; open 24 hours a day.

Terrace at the Osteria dell'Anima

FOOD AND DRINK

Any trip to Rome would be incomplete without trying some local delicacies. Expect lots of hearty pasta, grilled meats, delicate fish, decadent crispy artichokes and courgette flowers.

Italy is a land of regional cuisines, and while the names of well-known dishes are relatively similar throughout the country, the flavours are distinct. Rome is no exception, and restaurants of all classes and prices will generally offer their favourite local dishes. The delight of the Roman dish is in the simple combination of ingredients and in the careful preparation.

ORDER OF THE DAY

Generally Italians take a light breakfast of biscuits and coffee with milk. A mid-morning break is a must, and consists of a quick stop for a coffee and a *brioche*. A leisurely lunch is generally served between 1 and 3.30pm. The dinner hour starts at 8pm until 11.30pm or later.

Italian waiters believe in letting the diner enjoy a meal without feeling rushed. You may find yourself sitting for ages before anyone even looks in your direction. When you are ready to leave, simply request *il conto per favore* (the bill please); it's always wise to double-check it before you pay.

The menu
Traditional Italian menus have five full sections. They are arranged in the order in which they should be eaten, and dishes are served with a slight pause between each course. The menu starts with the *antipasto* (appetizer), followed by the *primo* (first course), consisting of either pasta, rice or soup. Next is the *secondo* (second course), or the meat, fish or poultry dish. Salads and vegetables are listed under *contorni* (side dishes). Seasonal vegetables do not always appear on the menu but they are usually available, and salads are never eaten before the main courses.

You don't have to order all the courses. For example, a pasta *primo* could be followed by a salad served in place of a *secondo*. The final dish is the *dolce* (dessert), with a digestive liqueur or an espresso at the end.

Roman cuisine is based on good hearty dishes and meats. Most menus will include some version of pasta with a salty pecorino cheese, such as *cacio e pepe* (cheese and freshly ground black pepper), *spaghetti all'amatriciana* (spicy tomato sauce with *guanciale*, a salt pork taken from the cheek), and pasta carbonara (creamy egg and cheese sauce seasoned with *guanciale*).

Meat counter at Volpetti   *Sweet treats at Dagnino*

PLACES TO EAT AND DRINK

Half the joy of Rome is to be found in its bustling restaurants, tiny cafés tucked between ancient monuments, and umbrella-covered tables spilling out into the streets. Food is a social event in this grand town.

Of the different restaurant types, a *ristorante* is the most formal. The goal of the meal at an *osteria* or *trattoria* is typically more casual, with the emphasis on good food not presentation and wine served in litre or half-litre carafes rather than bottles. Traditional wood-oven *pizzerie* serving thin-crust pizzas are not usually open for lunch, but a lunch version is available as *pizza al taglio* (by the slice), which is thicker and sold by weight.

Cafés and bars

Cafés are generally referred to in Italian as *bar*, which is actually the counter where coffees are served. In addition to coffee, they often serve aperitifs, cakes and pastries, and sandwiches. There are two listed prices at cafés – one for standing, and the other for table service. You will generally need to pay first at the till and bring the *scontrino* (receipt) to the barista to collect.

A basic coffee is a *caffè* (espresso), which can be adjusted by the addition of hot water for an americano, or varying amounts of steamed or frothed milk such as in a cappuccino or caffè latte. Milky coffees are considered breakfast drinks and are rarely ordered after 11am.

A caffè macchiato (stained coffee) is the appropriate replacement, consisting of an espresso with a dash of milk froth.

The great wines of Italy are generally available at any place where food is served. The best choices for wines are *enoteche* (wine bars), which often have extensive label selections and fantastic wines by the glass. They often open before dinner and serve light fare and tapas.

Pubs and clubs

A number of Irish pubs, serving beers and spirits and open until 1am, cater to the university crowd and to foreign visitors. These and several other pub-like bars can be found in Campo de' Fiori and between Piazza Navona and the Pantheon. Clubs also serve mixed drinks and are generally open quite late. The best sections for music and cocktails are in the Testaccio area or along Via Ostiense, while the more mellow or sophisticated clubs can be found around Piazza Navona. In the summer there are a number of open-air clubs in the parks and along the river.

Food and drink prices

Throughout this book, we have used the following price guide for a two-course meal for one with half a bottle of house wine.

€€€€ = €60 and above
€€€ = €40–60
€€ = €25–40
€ = under €25

Bulgari store on Via dei Condotti

SHOPPING

Rome is that rare thing – a city on the international shopping circuit that manages to keep small shops in business. While there is no shortage of fashion houses and cool boutiques, there are few ubiquitous high–street megastores.

Shopping in Rome still offers a few surprises if you have the courage to look. The most interesting shopping is found in neighbourhoods slightly off the beaten track, where you will find young designers, classic leather workers, made-to-measure tailors and other high-quality craftsmen, street markets and shops selling beautiful antiques.

MADE IN ROME

It is difficult to put a definitive stamp on what types of things are available in Rome. Leather goods, shoes, handmade papers and books, art prints, kitchenware and antiques tend to be the best bet for good-value shopping in the city. Each area has a delicatessen offering a good selection of wines and enticing home-cooked food tucked into their windows.

Just as likely are the shops displaying strings of postcards and calendars, plastic heads of Caesar and cheap 'Venetian' glass made in China; though next to these you may also find the one-off shop with something that you wouldn't be able to purchase in any other city. Several of the main districts can more or less be defined by their style.

In the touristy areas, most shops are generally open from 9/9.30am to 7.30/8pm. The larger department or chain stores will stay open through lunch (called *orario no-stop* or *orario continuato*), but family-run businesses and smaller shops mostly close between 1 and 3.30pm. Many shops close on Sunday and Monday, and very few stay open in August, although this is slowly changing.

WHERE TO FIND WHAT

Couture and elegance

If real fashion-house fashion is what you are after, then head for the Tridente. The small streets criss-crossing between the triangle of the Via del Corso and the Via del Babuino are home to the big names in couture and international designers. Here is where you will find the latest creations by Chanel, Fendi, Roberto Cavalli, La Perla, and the glittering jewels of Bulgari and Buccellati. Along the glamorous Via dei Condotti alone there is Gucci, Brioni, Prada, Louis Vuitton, Tiffany's and Valentino. The nearby Via Mario de' Fiori and the Via Bocca di

Silk ties in Trastevere   *Campo de' Fiori*

Leone have some smaller but just as recognisable designers.

Chic boutiques
Less elegant, less expensive and just as cool are Rome's boutiques. One-of-a-kind finds can be discovered in several locations. A good place to find the small designer scene is the neighbourhood of Monti. The shops along the Via del Boschetto are an interesting mix of slinky black dresses, cashmere in pretty colours, chunky arty jewellery and stylish items for the home. More boutiques and local designers can be found in Trastevere and on Via del Governo Vecchio and surrounding streets.

Similarly, the streets near Piazza Navona and the Pantheon have a long-standing tradition of boutique style. Via del Governo Vecchio and the Via Campo Marzio both have their own distinct flavour, with funky designs and classic understated elegance. Trastevere is home to a good number of traditional tailors and ethnic or club-orientated shops.

High-street and mainstream
For shops such as Nike, Diesel and Zara there is the jam-packed Via del Corso. Here you'll find all the familiar high-street names, high- and lower-end labels and all the books, music and trinkets you're after. Just around the corner is one of Rome's few department stores, La Rinascente. This is located across from the Art Nouveau-style Gal-

leria Alberto Sordi, which is essentially a small shopping mall.

A more pleasant version of Via del Corso is located in Prati, just a few streets away from the Vatican. The Via Cola di Rienzo is a wide boulevard lined with boutiques and cafés, the department store COIN and the speciality food shop Castroni.

For the younger crowd the Via dei Giubbonari, located between Campo de' Fiori and Via Arenula, is a great bet for inexpensive trends and the look of the minute.

Antiques
The Via dei Coronari is where to go for antiques. This elegant street has shops spilling out onto the pavement with some wonderful Italian furniture and paintings. In May and October antiques fairs are held here. The Via del Babuino comes in second for high-end pieces. For bargains the area of Monti has some good affordable finds, or real junk-hunting can be done at the Sunday Porta Portese street market in Trastevere (6am–2pm).

Food markets
A great place to pick up picnic provisions is at one of Rome's colourful food markets. The best known is on Piazza di Campo de' Fiori, but others include Piazza Mastai in Trastevere, Piazza dell'Unitá in Prati, the Nuovo Mercato Esquilino in Via Turati and the Testaccio market in Via A. Volta. Markets are generally open Mon–Sat 7am–2pm.

Opera performance in a church setting

ENTERTAINMENT

Entertaining the masses has been an important feature in the fabric of Roman life since ancient times. The social element is what keeps the locals happy, and they ensure there is always something new to do.

As with any major metropolitan city, there is an abundance of choice when it comes to entertainment in Rome. Whether you would prefer to see a modern play, dance to techno on the beach, or hear a Stradivarius played in a Baroque church, Rome has it all. Connecting these seemingly unrelated activities is what the Italians call '*la bella figura*' (making a good impression or being just right). This concept of elegant appropriateness is visible in, for example, the setting of a fashion show within a Renaissance hall or a modern dance performance in an archaeological excavation. Entertainment for Romans often juxtaposes traditional with trendy elements. This, plus the potential of hosting open-air events for seven months of the year, makes for a rich cultural city with an ever-changing list of 'what's on'.

Once you have decided on what type of pursuit takes your fancy, the next step is to find out what is happening and when. A good first stop is at a PIT tourist kiosk (see page 130) for up-to-date information on nearly every activity possible. The City Council (Comune di Roma) publishes *A Guest in Rome* (www.unospitearoma.it), an excellent free monthly guide with listings of concerts, ballet, exhibitions, museum schedules, theatre, markets and children's activities. The main papers, such as *La Repubblica* or *Il Messaggero*, publish daily event listings, but only in Italian.

Roman's take great entertainment in the *passeggiata*, or leisurely stroll. Before dinner or a big night out, you will see people of all ages engaging in this pastime. This is not just a form of social exercise, but a chance to see and be seen. Italians will often be in their best threads for public display.

THEATRE

One of the oldest art forms in Rome is theatre. The vibrant contemporary scene has come a long way from the tragedy and satire of antiquity. While there is no Broadway-style venue, the city is home to nearly 80 national and independent stages. Productions range from large-scale in Teatro Argentina to experimental performances in Teatro India, both run by the city council. Most productions are

Drinks with a view

in Italian only. However, smaller English companies do exist such as the English Theatre of Rome.

MUSIC AND DANCE

Opera

The city's main opera house is the opulent Teatro dell'Opera (www.oper aroma.it), which stages big production operas and ballets. Opera fans will also be enticed by performances within the ruins of the Baths of Caracalla (see page 37), as part of the Teatro dell'Opera's summer season. Opera is also performed in smaller theatres and churches across the city.

Other music and dance

The Auditorium Parco della Musica (see page 122) (www.auditorium.com) ensures a continually changing programme of performing arts in the city's best concert venue. Everything from superb classical orchestras to big blues and pop stars can be enjoyed here. The world-class music academy of Santa Cecilia has a dedicated music hall inside the Auditorium. In recent years, multicultural music has made a serious debut in form of the Orchestra di Piazza Vittorio (www.orchestradipiazzavittorio. it), with musicians assembled from ten countries playing classical music on traditional instruments.

In addition to ballet, vibrant modern dance performances are showcased at a number of annual festivals in Rome.

FESTIVALS

During Estate Romana, thousands of events from fashion shows to world music to circus acts take place across the city. Roma Europa (www.romae uropa.net; Sep–Nov) is more cutting edge, with contemporary art and performance. For film buffs, there's the Roma Cinema Fest (www.romacine mafest.it) in October, plus the open-air cinemas at Piazza Vittorio and Isola Tiberina (June–Aug); for fashionistas, there is the Alta Roma Alta Moda (www. altaroma.it; Jan and July), Rome's version of fashion week. For world music lovers there is the Rome Meets the World Festival in Villa Ada (www.vil laada.org) from June to July.

NIGHTLIFE

Roman nightlife starts late. Don't expect much to be happening at weekends or in summer before 11pm. Beyond the ubiquitous glass of wine at an *eno teca*, Rome has a number of popular pubs and funky bars catering to a student crowd. These get lively in the wee hours around the Campo de' Fiori area and parts of Trastevere. For a more subdued cocktail vibe, there are a number of clubs near Piazza Navona. Testaccio and Ostiense have the greatest selection of full on *discoteche*, with house DJs and dance floors. Many of these close in the heat of the summer and move to their beach locations at Ostia.

Model of Imperial Rome, Museo della Civiltà Romana

MUSEUMS

Rome is often referred to as the city of museums. At times the whole city seems like one vast open–air museum; nowhere else in the world is there such a varied collection of artistic treasures in such a compact space.

While some visitors are happy with a day spent picking through the ruins of the Roman Forum, imagining the gladiators at the Colosseum, or elbowing their way into the Sistine Chapel, others will want to delve deeper into Rome's rich cultural heritage.

Opening times

Many State- and City-run museums are closed on Mondays. Private museums will often compensate for this by closing on either Sunday or Tuesday. The Vatican Museums are closed on Sunday. Opening times are seasonal and may be subject to last-minute changes, so it's worth checking in advance.

COMBINATION TICKETS

The City of Rome has set up combination tickets for some museums, providing substantial savings.

The **Roma Pass** (www.romapass.it) is an excellent choice for savings. It comes as a kit, which includes a map, a three-day pass for unlimited bus and metro use, and free entry to the first two museums or sites you visit (including any special exhibitions), and reduced entry to all the others, as well as discounts for shops and restaurants.. Over 45 monuments, museums, and archaeological sites participate in the Roma Pass.

The **Roma Archeologia Card** (www.coopculture.it) is valid for seven days and gives entry into all of the sites under the care of the Roman National Museums. These are the Roman Forum, Palatine Hill, Colosseum, Baths of Caracalla, Baths of Diocletian, Palazzo Massimo alle Terme, Palazzo Altemps, Crypta Balbi and the Tomb of Cecilia Metella. It does not include public transportation.

Tickets for the Capitoline Museums also include entry into the sister collection at the Centrale Montemartini (valid for seven days), while tickets for the Vatican Collections include entry into the Vatican Historical Museum at San Giovanni in Laterano, if used within five days of purchase.

Tickets for the Roman Forum also grant entry to the Colosseum and the Palatine Hill.

ADDITIONAL MUSEUMS

There are a number of wonderful, interesting or plain quirky museums not

Classical statuary   *The glorious Vatican*

included in the walking tours. A selection of some of the best follows:

Archaeology

Case Romane (Roman Houses of the Celio Hill; Clivo di Scauro; www.case romane.it; Thu–Mon 10am–6pm, Tue–Wed 10am–2pm; charge, with advance reservation). Over 20 frescoes from the 2nd and 3rd centuries in a lovely setting.

Crypta Balbi (Via delle Botteghe Oscure 31; Tue–Sun 9am–7.45pm). Combining state-of-the-art technology with dramatic ruins, this museum traces the development of Roman society.

Fine arts

Galleria Colonna (Piazza SS Apostoli; www.galleriacolonna.it; Sat only 9am–1.15pm). The Colonna collection rivals those of the Doria Pamphilj and Palazzo Barberini.

MAXXI (National Museum of the 21st-Century Arts; Via Guido Reni 4a; www.maxxi.art; Tue–Fri and Sun 11am–7pm, Sat 11am–10pm). Zaha Hadid-designed space for contemporary art and architecture.

Museo Barracco (Corso Vittorio Emanuele 166; www.museobarracco.it; Oct–May Tue–Sun 10am–4pm, June–Sep 1–7pm). An elegant Renaissance palace houses this prestigious collection of ancient sculpture.

Palazzo Altemps (48 Piazza di Sant' Apollinare; Tue–Sun 9am–7.45pm). Set around a courtyard, this delightful museum contains many treasures of Classical statuary and art from the National Roman Museums' collection.

History

Museo Napoleonico (Piazza di Ponte Umberto I, 1, www.museonapoleon ico.it, Tue–Sun 10am–6pm). This museum traces the history of the Napoleonic era through paintings and sculptures that document the intense relationships between Rome and the Bonapartes.

Museo Nazionale delle Arti e Tradizioni Popolari (National Museum of Folk Arts and Traditions; Piazza Marconi 8, EUR; www.muse ocivilta.beniculturali.it; Tue–Sun 8am–7pm). A lively display of Rome's social history through folk art, costumes and more.

Unusual collections

Explora Children's Museum (Via Flaminia 82; www.mdbr.it; Tue–Sun 10am–6.45pm). Bring the children here when they are tired of ancient Rome; lots of buttons to press and levers to pull.

Museo Criminologico (Museum of Criminology; Via del Gonfalone 29; www.museocriminologico.it; Tue–Sat 9am–1pm, Tue and Thu 2.30–6.30pm). Teenagers may enjoy this interesting collection of crime-related items, which include a section on mafia and organized crime and one on torture instruments.

'Roman senate in session' by Cesare Maccari

HISTORY: KEY DATES

Emperors and popes, dictators and rebels, philosophers and barbarians, saints and sinners; from immense wealth to pillage and ruin, Romans really have seen it all.

FOUNDING OF THE REPUBLIC

753 BC According to legend, Romulus founds Rome.

509 Fall of the Etruscan king, Tarquinius Superbus. Republic founded.

450 Roman law is codified.

390 Gauls plunder Rome.

312 Appius Claudius starts the Appian Way.

241 Victory in the First Punic War.

218 Second Punic War. Hannibal crosses the Alps.

146 Carthage and Corinth destroyed.

133 Civil war starts with the murder of Tiberius Gracchus.

100 Birth of Julius Caesar.

71 Gladiator revolt led by Spartacus ends in bloodbath.

60 First triumvirate: Caesar, Pompey, Crassus.

51 Julius Caesar conquers Gaul, crosses the Rubicon.

44 Caesar assassinated.

43 Second triumvirate: Antony, Octavian, Aemilius Lepidus.

31 Caesar Octavian Augustus defeats Mark Antony at Actium.

THE ROMAN EMPIRE

27 BC Caesar Augustus assumes autocracy, establishes Pax Romana.

41 AD Caligula assassinated. Claudius accedes.

64 Great fire, and persecution of early Christians under Nero.

67 St Peter martyred.

80 Construction of Colosseum.

98 Empire expanded to Persia under Trajan.

125 Construction of Pantheon under Hadrian.

270 Aurelian builds defensive walls.

286 Diocletian divides empire between east and west.

312 Constantine defeats Maxentius. Establishes Christianity.

330 Constantinople made new capital of the empire.

410 Rome plundered and aqueducts destroyed under Alaric the Goth.

Depiction of the election of Pope Pius II, 1458, by Pinturicchio

MEDIEVAL ROME, RENAISSANCE AND REPUBLIC

476   Last western emperor abdicates. Byzantium made seat of Empire.

800   Coronation of Charlemagne as Holy Roman Emperor.

1300   Pope Boniface VIII establishes the first Holy Year.

1309   Clement V abandons Rome, and moves papacy to Avignon.

1377   Papacy returns to Rome under Gregory XI.

1417   The election of Martin V ends 40 years of papal schism.

1503   Pope Julius II starts work on the new St Peter's (the building is finally consecrated in 1626).

1527   The Great Sack of Rome under German and Spanish troops.

1545   Initiation of the Council of Trent and Counter-Reformation.

1797   Napoleon Bonaparte makes Rome a republic, and exiles the Pope.

19TH CENTURY TO THE PRESENT DAY

1815   The Roman Church state is restored by Congress of Vienna.

1849   Revolutionary establishment of new Roman Republic.

1870   Rome is made capital of the newly unified Italy. City renovation begins.

1922   Fascists march on Rome. Mussolini becomes dictator.

1929   Lateran Treaty creates Vatican State.

1944   Allied troops liberate the city.

1957   The Treaty of Rome is signed – the foundation for a united Europe.

1960   Rome hosts the Olympic Games. Period of 'La Dolce Vita'.

2001   Media magnate Silvio Berlusconi is elected Prime Minister for the first time.

2005   Pope John Paul II dies. Cardinal Ratzinger is elected Pope Benedict XVI.

2011   Berlusconi resigns amid the euro crisis. He is succeeded by technocratic PM Mario Monti.

2013   Mayor Ignazio Marino turns the Colosseo and Fori Imperiali street into a pedestrian area.

2015   In October, Marino is forced to resign following intense pressure from his party (PD).

2016   Virginia Raggi, of the Five Star Movement, becomes the first woman to be elected mayor of Rome.

2018   The Five Star Movement wins the most seats in the general election but not an overall majority. A coalition is formed between League and the Five Star Movement.

2019   Assessment of figures show Italy crept back into recession towards the end of 2018.

2020   Rome is one of 12 cities selected to host the UEFA Euro 2020 tournament.

BEST ROUTES

Statue in the Musei Capitolini

CAPITOLINE HILL AND ROMAN FORUM

The area between the Capitoline Hill and Colosseum has long been seen as the civic centre of Rome. This route covers some of the city's key museums, then follows the Via Sacra through Rome's oldest neighbourhood to Trajan's Markets.

DISTANCE: 4.5km (2.75 miles)
TIME: A full day
START: Piazza Venezia
END: Trajan's Markets
POINTS TO NOTE: More than a dozen buses stop at Piazza Venezia. While this walking route is actually quite contained, there is a lot to see. There are few places to stop for a break along the way, so a bottle of water and good walking shoes are recommended.

If all roads lead to Rome, then all roads in Rome seem to lead to **Piazza Venezia**, the hub of the city's road network since 1881. The square is dominated by the extravagant **Monumento a Vittorio Emanuele II ❶**, or 'Il Vittoriano', inaugurated in 1911 and intended to honour the newly unified Italy – although actually dedicated to the first King of the Republic, Victor Emmanuel II. Its construction was fraught with controversy, as large sums of the newly imposed national taxes were funnelled into the project, and sections of the ancient Capitoline Hill and surround-ing neighbourhoods were demolished to create space. Italians refer to the monument as the 'wedding cake' or 'typewriter'. It is topped by a bronze equestrian figure of the king, and the Eternal Flame of the Fatherland and the Tomb of the Unknown Soldier are located on the front step. From the monument, walk south along the Via del Teatro di Marcello and then take the second stairway on the left.

CAMPIDOGLIO

The harmonious **Piazza del Campi-doglio ❷** is located at the top of the Cap-itoline Hill, which rises majestically above the nearby Forum and city centre, and was once home to the important temple of Jupiter Optimus Maximus Capitolinus. The ancient Tabularium (office of records and archives) built in 78 BC stands at the south side of the piazza in what is now called the **Palazzo Senatorio**. It still houses the city records offices of the local government.

Michelangelo's design

The current look of the piazza dates from the Renaissance and is primarily the

Capitoline Hill

Foro Romano

design of Michelangelo. Pope Paul III Farnese commissioned the remodelling of the space in celebration of the visit of Holy Roman Emperor Charles V, scheduled for 1538. His plan included the reworking of the stairs and the piazza to showcase the equestrian statue of Marcus Aurelius of 80 AD (an excellent copy

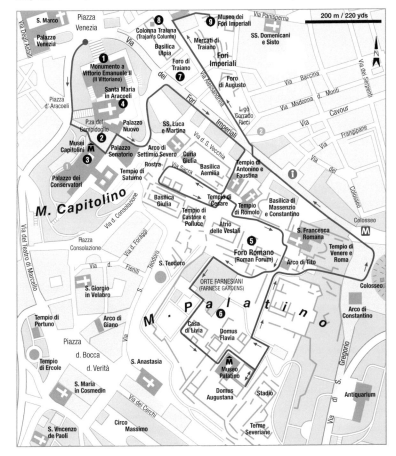

'Dying Gaul', Musei Capitolini

now stands in the piazza). Michelangelo also changed the orientation of the government buildings by turning them away from the Classical Forum to face the Vatican. The two elegant palaces on either side of the piazza house the important collections of the Musei Capitolini.

Capitoline Museums

The entrance to the **Musei Capitolini ❸** (Piazza del Campidoglio 1; www.musei capitolini.org; daily 9.30am–7.30pm) is on the southwest side of the piazza in the **Palazzo dei Conservatori**. It is considered the oldest public sculpture collection in the world and was founded in 1471 by Pope Sixtus IV (better known for commissioning the Sistine Chapel). The palace courtyard contains the remains of a statue of Emperor Constantine. In the first-floor galleries are some of Rome's most famous treasures, including the statue of the 5th century BC she-wolf suckling the infants Romulus and Remus, the classic *Thorn Puller*, and Emperor Commodus posing as *Hercules*. The original statue of Marcus Aurelius is in the atrium. Many of the rooms are decorated with works by Pietro da Cortona and frescoes by Cavaliere d'Arpino. The upper-level galleries showcase paintings by Guido Reni, Caravaggio, Tintoretto, Titian and Veronese.

Take the underground passage through the Tabularium, to the **Palazzo Nuovo** collection on the opposite side. Here are some of the best examples of ancient sculpture. On the first floor are statues including the *Cupid and Psyche*, the *Dying Gaul* copied from a 3rd-century BC original, and the luscious *Capitoline Venus*. The rare collection of portrait busts of emperors and philosophers is displayed chronologically.

If refreshments are needed there is a nice **museum café**, see ❶, inside the Palazzo Caffarelli, which is behind the Palazzo dei Conservatori.

Santa Maria in Aracoeli

Sharing the top of the Capitoline Hill is the 12th-century church of **Santa Maria in Aracoeli ❹**. A long staircase, north of Michelangelo's grand stairway, leads to this lovely church which is still designated Church of the Roman city council. The climb up is worth the effort for a look at the interior, with oil lamps, sparkling mosaics, Cosmati floors, and 22 columns from nearby pagan temples.

ROMAN FORUM

Take the street at the left of Palazzo Senatorio to descend the Capitoline. From here there are sweeping views over the area generally referred to as the **Foro Romano ❺** (Roman Forum). The main Forum sits in the valley created by the Palatine, Esquiline and Capitoline hills and served as the political, civic and religious centre of ancient Rome for a period lasting over a thousand years. Rome became a republic in 509 BC, and the last monument to be erected in the area was the Column of the Byzantine Emperor Phocas, added in 608 AD. The majestic remains of

Tabularium   *Basilica of St Mary of the Altar of Heaven*

the Roman Empire still dominate the centre of Rome, even in their current form as a heavily visited archaeological park.

Sacred Way

To enter the site, walk down the hill to the Via dei Fori Imperiali (a straight, parade-friendly boulevard created in 1932 by Mussolini by bulldozing medieval districts, Renaissance towers and vast sections of the Fora) to the **main entrance** of the Roman Forum and Palatine Hill (Via della Salara Vecchia, 5/6, entrance also at Via di San Gregorio 30; www.coopculture.it; daily from 8.30am, closing times vary seasonally; tickets are valid for two days for the Forum, Palatine Hill and Colosseum). If there is a queue, try the ticket area on Via di San Gregorio and start from the Palatine Hill.

What looks like a disorderly collection of ruins was once a magnificent city of temples, shops, courts and triumphal arches, connected by broad streets. The area survived several major restructures, and the additional Imperial Fora extended to the Forum of Caesar, Forum of Augustus, and the expansive Forum of Trajan. Entering the site along the **Via Sacra** (Sacred Way), takes you through the middle of the archaeological area of the Roman Forum.

Senate House

To the right of the main entrance, heading northwest along the Via Sacra, are the remains of the **Basilica Aemilia**, a 2nd-century BC meeting hall for traders and commerce. Just past it is the **Curia Giulia** (Senate House) designed to hold up to 200 senators. The original 7th-century BC structure was rebuilt four times after it was destroyed by fire. The current structure dates from 283 AD under Emperor Diocletian.

Arch of Septimius Severus

The path leads past the triumphal **Arco di Settimio Severo** (Arch of Septimius Severus) constructed in 203 AD. The triple arch was built in celebration of the victory over the Parthians (modern Iran) and still displays carved reliefs depicting scenes from the battle. Across from the arch is the **Rostra** (Speaker's Platform), built for public announcements. It is from here, in Shakespeare's Julius Caesar, that Marc Antony makes his famous 'Friends, Romans, countrymen, lend me your ears…' speech.

Temple of Saturn

Nearby are the massive Ionic columns with a section of frieze. It is all that remains of the **Tempio di Saturno**, first built in 498 BC to house the *Aerarium* (state treasury), and was the most venerated temple in the Forum.

The flat area with column bases is the **Basilica Giulia**, home to the civil courts. Some steps still have the remnants of games of marbles inscribed in the stone. On the far side you will see three fluted columns from the **Il Tempio dei Dioscuri** (Temple to Castor and Pollux), next to an unassuming metal roof marking the **Tem-**

Temple of Saturn

pio di Cesare (Temple of Caesar). It was here that the great leader's body was brought after his death.

Temple of Antoninus and Faustina

Back along the Via Sacra you will pass the **Tempio di Antonino e Faustina** (Temple of Antoninus and Faustina), which was converted into a church in the 12th century. Beyond is the circular **Tempio di Romolo** (Temple of Romulus) with its magnificent original bronze doors from 309 AD. The temple was likely part of the Forum of Peace, and was incorporated into the early Christian church of Saints Cosmos and Damian. The interior can be seen from the church (on Via dei Fori Imperiali). Opposite the doors is the path to the **Atrio delle Vestali** (House of the Vestal Virgins) with the colonnade of the courtyard and the circular temple. Here the Vestal Virgins kept the sacred flame of Rome burning.

Just up a low hill are the brick remains of the **Basilica di Massenzio e Constantino** (Basilica of Maxentius and Constantine), dating from 303. The three arches indicate only the side section of the structure.

Arch of Titus

At the far end of the Via Sacra is the **Arco di Tito** (Arch of Titus). The triumphal arch was constructed in 82 AD to mark the sack of Jerusalem a decade earlier by the forces of Vespasian and Titus. The carved reliefs depict the figure of Roma with Titus, and a distinct processional of the spoils of the war. The treasures include the altar and Menorah from the temple of Solomon.

Palatine Hill

Next to the Arch of Titus is the entrance to the **Monte Palatino ❻** (Palatine Hill), the oldest inhabited part of Rome. Supposedly, it was on the Palatine that the twins Romulus and Remus were found in the cave of the Lupercal (She-wolf). This hill has long been home to notable Romans, including Caesar Augustus, Cicero and Marc Antony, and many palace remains can still be found here. Much of the Palatine was reworked during the Renaissance when it was bought by Cardinal Alessandro Farnese and turned into a fine garden.

The **Orti Farnesiani** (Farnese Gardens) dominate the central area of the hill. Here a subterranean vaulted passageway leads to the **Casa di Livia** (House of Livia), the best-preserved house in the Forum area.

South of the gardens lies the **Domus Flavia**, built by Emperor Domitian. The grey building sandwiched between this and the **Domus Augustana** is the **Museo Palatino** (same hours as main complex), housing a collection of artefacts from the ongoing excavations. Nearby is the **Stadio** (Stadium), and beyond are the ruins of the **Terme Severiane** (Baths of Septimius Severus), with aqueducts. Below is the **Circo Massimo** (see page 37).

Exit the Palatino and Forum Romanum from the Via Sacra at the Col-

Trajan's Market

osseum. Tickets allow entry into this section of the archaeological site for two days. Now take the Via dei Fori Imperiali, past the **Visitor Information Centre** along the right, to the Via Alessandrina. If a break is needed, try the **Enoteca Cavour 313**, see ❷.

TRAJAN'S FORUM

The raised walk makes a nice path above the remains of the **Foro di Traiano** ❼ (Trajan's Forum). This monumental complex, started by Emperor Trajan in 106, extended along the Quirinale to the Capitoline Hill. Sections of the exedra are still visible along the arched curve of the lower markets. The remains of the basilica Ulpia can be seen on the left, and at the far end is the **Colonna Traiana** ❽ (Trajan's Column).

This 38m (125ft) -high victory symbol was erected in 113 in honour of Trajan's triumph over the Dacians. The column is in excellent condition given its age, but the original painted details have been lost. The elaborate relief carving depicts scenes from the battle, spiralling 23 times around the column from the ground upward. The statue of St Peter was added in 1587, replacing the original bronze of Trajan. The Emperor's remains were placed in the base of the column after his death.

Trajan's Market
Walk up the nearby stairs to the Via IV Novembre, the entrance of the **Mercati di Traiano** and **Museo dei Fori**

Imperiali ❾ (Trajan's Market and Museum of Imperial Fora; Via IV Novembre 94; www.mercatiditraiano.it; daily 9.30am–7.30pm). Here, you can walk along the old stalls that sold wines, seafood, vegetables, fruit and oil. The lower floors had space for offices and granaries, and even a tavern. The complex houses reliefs and some of the best-preserved architecture of the Forum and often hosts contemporary art exhibits.

The remains of the Fori Imperiali lie on either side and buried beneath the Via dei Fori Imperiali. As Rome grew in power, its population increased, and the original Roman Forum was no longer big enough to serve the city's needs. The Imperial Fora were built by a succession of emperors from Caesar to Trajan.

Food and drink

❶ CAFFE CAPITOLINO
Palazzo dei Conservatori on the Caffarelli Terrace; tel: 06-6919 0564; daily 9.30am–7pm; €
The museum café is perfect for a quick bite or a drink. Terrace has superb views.

❷ ENOTECA CAVOUR 313
Via Cavour 313; tel: 06-678 5496; https://cavour313.it; daily 12.30pm–2.45pm, Mon–Thu 6–11pm, Fri–Sat 6pm–midnight; €€
Enoteca with a great wine selection and excellent seasonal menu.

The iconic Colosseum

THE COLOSSEUM

This route starts at the Colosseum, the enduring symbol of Rome, and makes a wide circle along the less-visited side of the Forum to take in the grandiose remains of some of the Eternal City's best-preserved temples and monuments, located along the river.

DISTANCE: 3.5km (2 miles)
TIME: A half day
START: Colosseum
END: Theatre of Marcellus
POINTS TO NOTE: Buses 51, 75, 85, and 87, and metro B Colosseo stop in front of the Colosseum. Tickets for it are combined with the Forum and Palatine Hill, and can be used again within a 48-hour period. There are few choices for food and drink between the Colosseum and the Circus Maximus, so bring a snack and a drink. Children generally enjoy this route, although you may have to break it up, as it is quite long.

THE COLOSSEUM

The route starts outside the **Colosseo** ❶ (Colosseum; Piazza del Colosseo; www.coopculture.it; 8.30am–1 hour before sunset; entrances also at Via di San Gregorio 30 and Via dei Fori Imperiali; tickets valid for two days for the Forum, Palatine Hill and Colosseum), in the Piazza del Colosseo,

and continues to the far side of the Palatine hill.

The amphitheatre was commissioned by the Emperor Vespasian in 72 AD to host the brutal but popular gladiatorial games and animal combat. Despite its condition it still remains an absolutely awe-inspiring sight.

History

The Colosseum was built over the site of Emperor Nero's artificial lake. Originally named the Amphitheatrum Flavium (Flavian Amphitheatre), it was given the nickname the Colosseum because of its proximity to the Colossus of Nero. A bronze-and-gilt statue once stood in front of the amphitheatre, reaching up to the fourth floor. Part of the statue's base is still visible near the Via Sacra.

The ingenious design of the amphitheatre allowed for easy access of up to 55,000 people, and the entire arena could be emptied of spectators in less than 10 minutes using all 80 arched entrances. The top of the Colosseum could be covered with a huge canvas awning shading spectators and con-

The defining image of Rome   *Inside the Colosseum*

testants from the sun. However, the biggest draw of the Colosseum was not the architecture, but the games.

Deadly purpose

The gladiator games and exotic animal fights were free of charge to the public. Events were often theatrical to lighten the gruesome nature of the real entertainment. The fights always ended in death, and a constant supply of animals and men was needed to keep the system going. Gladiators were pitted against gladiators, animals against gladiator, and animal against animal. Around 5,000 wild animals were slaughtered in the first 100 days of the games when the stadium first opened in 80 AD. While expensively trained gladiators were often spared death, animals and slaves never were. The brutal games were eventually banned in 523 AD.

Structure

What we now see from the main piazza are the skeletal remains of the once-grand structure. The exposed brickwork

is merely the inner support wall. Most of the magnificently carved decoration and massive block were stripped from the building and used for the construction of St Peter's and Renaissance palaces. The ransacking of raw materials continued until the 18th century, when

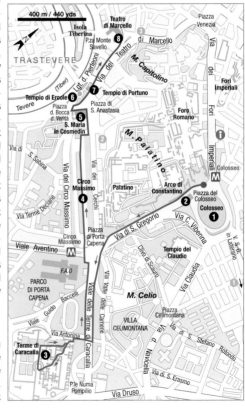

Arch of Constantine

Pope Benedict XIV consecrated it as a church. Major architectural reconstruction and restoration has been carried out since the 20th century to keep the building standing. Some of the decoration is still visible on the side facing the Via dei Imperiali.

How the Colosseum worked

The view from the inside shows an open brickwork area under what was once a wooden-floored arena. The floor could be covered with sand and raked between games to 'clean' the arena, and it hid a series of trapdoors that opened to the rooms and animal cages below (now exposed). The seating is only visible in a few sections where marble block remains. Seating was organised in a complicated division of status and social class, and was often dependent on who was hosting the game. The best view of the internal structure is from the upper floors looking back down into the Colosseum. Exits are located at the north and west sides.

If you're ready to eat, take the north side exit and walk a few minutes east into the nearby neighbourhood of the Celio. Along the Via di San Giovanni in Laterano is the **Hostaria Isidoro**, see ❶, serving a great-value lunch or dinner.

To continue the walk, follow the black paving stones from the west exit to the Arch of Constantine, dominating the south side of the Piazza del Colosseo.

ARCH OF CONSTANTINE

The **Arco di Constantino** ❷ was the last great triumphal arch to be constructed in the Roman Forum. It was erected in 315 by the Emperor Constantine I just before the shift of political power moved from Rome to Byzantium. Most of the magnificently carved decoration is made from 'recycled' scenes taken from other nearby monuments. The arch commemorates the Christian Emperor's battle against Maxentius at the Milvian Bridge, where he fought under the sign of the cross.

Rome vs Byzantium

When Emperor Constantine I came to power in the 4th century, the Roman Empire was already fragmented and overstretched. Constantine worked to unify some of the diversity in politics and religion, and established Christianity as an official religion at the Edict of Milan. At the time, Christianity was seen as one of many mystical cults, and was much more popular in the east than in Rome. Constantine worked on spreading the Empire between two major cities, with Rome governing the west and Byzantium governing the east. He eventually moved the capital city to the more Christian-friendly Byzantium. The new capital was renamed Constantinople (now Istanbul), and Rome was effectively left to decay. It was not long before the great palaces and temples were sacked by invaders.

Inside the Baths of Caracalla

Towards the Baths of Caracalla

Walking past the arch along the Via di San Gregorio, and passing under a remaining section of aqueduct, you will come to an intersection at the Piazza di Porta Capena. Cross left at the lights, and continue along the tree-lined Viale delle Terme di Caracalla. Cross right at the Via Antonina and up the path to the entrance of the archaeological complex.

BATHS OF CARACALLA

The massive brick remains of the bath complex of the **Terme di Caracalla** ❸ (Viale delle Terme di Caracalla 52; www.coopculture.it; Mon 9am–2pm, Tue–Sun 9am–1 hour before sunset) are a testament to what was once the world's largest leisure centre. Construction of the 11-hectare (27-acre) complex was started in 212 under the Emperor Caracalla. The baths, or *thermae*, were the ultimate statement of the architectural achievements of the Empire. The facilities could accommodate up to 1,600 people and in addition to the baths, saunas, gymnasia and massage rooms, there were spaces for lectures, shopping, art galleries and a comprehensive library. The largest rooms were the gymnasia.

Bathing ritual

The important ritual of Roman bathing included first a dip in the hot caldarium, followed by the cooler tepidarium, then a plunge into the cold frigidarium, and finally a swim in the large pool, or *natatio*.

Under the floor tiles was a massive labyrinth of water pipes, tunnels and heat conduits that were constantly maintained to keep the steam rooms and baths at the correct temperatures. The complex was used continuously for over 300 years, and was finally closed in 537, after the Visigoths sacked Rome and destroyed the aqueducts. Some of the matching sets of columns from the poolside portico can be seen holding up the nave of Santa Maria in Trastevere (see page 75), and two of the great decorative basins now adorn the Piazza Farnese (see page 44).

CIRCUS MAXIMUS

Exit left from the baths, head northwest along the Viale delle Terme di Caracalla, passing the ominous-looking FAO building (the Food and Agriculture Organization for the United Nations); cross the Viale Aventino and you will reach the **Circo Massimo** ❹ (Circus Maximus).

Like many of Rome's ancient monuments the giant space of the circus is larger than legend. Dating to the 6th century BC the grand outdoor arena hosted sporting events for nearly 1,000 years. The original stadium held over 250,000 spectators, and the main attraction was the dangerous four-horse chariot race. The *spina* (centre spine) would have been raised and decorated with small temple-like structures and obelisks, attesting to the strengths and prowess of various athletes. Almost nothing remains of the original stadium structure, though green

hillside at the left edge alludes to the seating. Some bits of brickwork at the southern edge are all that is left of the building.

Today the Circus Maximus is used as a park and picnic area. It is perfect for an early morning jog or cycling. Occasionally the space is used for concerts and sporting events.

FORUM BOARIUM

Crossing the Circus Maximus, exit at the north corner of Via dell'Ara Massimo di Ercole and the Via dei Cerchi. You should find the delightful old-fashioned trattoria, **Alvaro al Circo Massimo**, see ②, a great place for a traditional Roman long lunch or dinner.

Continue along the Via dei Cerchi, and turn left at the traffic-filled piazza. This low-lying area along the river is generally known as the **Forum Boarium** and was once used as the cattle market for ancient Rome.

Mouth of Truth

On the left is the church of **Santa Maria in Cosmedin** ❺ (Piazza della Bocca della Verità; daily 9.30am–6pm, until 5pm in winter). Inside the covered entrance to the 6th-century church is the Bocca della Verità (Mouth of Truth). There is often a queue, as visitors are requested to leave a donation and approach the mouth one by one. This carving has a long history of use as a lie detector, dating back to the Middle Ages. Legend has it that if you place

your hand in its mouth, and have not been completely truthful, your hand will be bitten off. The carving was likely originally made as a decorative manhole cover or drainage for a rain gutter. The Bocca della Verità was made popular in the 1953 film *Roman Holiday* starring Gregory Peck and Audrey Hepburn.

The church itself is pleasingly simple, with a nice mixture of medieval and Romanesque decoration. The Cosmati floors are original, and at the far left there are some relics of St Valentine, always popular with young lovers.

Temples of Hercules and Portunus

Across the piazza are two lovely temples that are among the oldest in the city. The round temple dates to the 2nd century BC and is thought to have been dedicated to Hercules. For many years the **Tempio di Ercole** ❻ (can be visited on the third Sunday of the month) was mistakenly considered the temple of Vesta because of its circular structure. The columns are in remarkable condition considering their age.

The rectangular temple across the piazza is dedicated to **Portunus** ❼, the god who served as gatekeeper of the granary stores, and of the ports and harbours. The location of the temple along the Tiber banks is near the ancient market port, and it was likely erected in an auspicious position of protection. The temple is on its original base, giving a sense of the original height. The fluted columns and triangular pediment remain amazingly intact.

Circus Maximus

THEATRE OF MARCELLUS

The winding Via del Teatro di Marcello will bring you to **Teatro di Marcello** ❽ (Via del Portico d'Ottavia 29; daily 9am–6pm, until 7pm in summer). The once-regal performance space of the theatre dates to the last years of the 1st century BC. It is named after Marcellus, Emperor Augustus's nephew, who died at age 19. The area was originally cleared for construction by Julius Caesar, although, ironically, Caesar was murdered in the nearby Theatre of Pompey before it could be built. The architectural plan was elegant and included three full seating levels, holding 20,000 visitors.

Much of the decorative marble was removed to construct other buildings, and the empty spaces within the arches and supports were filled in with medieval buildings. The far side of the archaeological walk opens onto the main piazza of the Jewish ghetto, providing views of the opposite side. Nearby are three standing Corinthian columns that originally came from the Temple of Apollo in Greece.

Consider finishing the walk with a gelato or cold drink at the **Antico Caffè**, see ❸, a family-run business just opposite the entrance of the Teatro di Marcello, with umbrella-covered tables overlooking the theatre ruins.

Food and drink

① HOSTARIA ISIDORO

Via San Giovanni in Laterano 59; tel: 06-700 8266; www.hostariaisidoro.com; Sun–Thu noon–11pm, Friday until 11.30pm, Sat 6–11.30pm; €

Built in a 17th-century cloister, this restaurant offers a rare combination – good food and excellent value near the Colosseum. You can tell the food is top notch because the restaurant is usually packed out with Romans. Try the tasting menu, or the wonderful seafood risotto; other classics include tagliatelle with artichokes and spaghetti with clams.

② ALVARO AL CIRCO MASSIMO

Via di S. Teodoro 89; tel: 06-678 6112;

Tue–Sat 12.30–3.30pm, 7–11.30pm, Sun 12.30–3.30pm; €€

This pleasantly old-fashioned trattoria with a homely atmosphere serves a lovely selection of traditional Roman dishes. It is generally packed with local government officials, and is best known for fish dishes and seasonal grilled porcini.

③ ANTICO CAFFÈ DEL TEATRO MARCELLO

Via del Teatro di Marcello 42; tel: 06-678 5451; 7am–11pm; €

This family-run café makes fresh sandwiches daily. Try one of their excellent coffees, homemade pastries or a cold freshly squeezed orange juice, served at a street-side table.

Fountain of the Four Rivers, Piazza Navona

PIAZZA NAVONA TO CAMPO DE' FIORI

The adjoining areas of Piazza Navona and Campo de' Fiori make two halves of the old medieval city centre. The winding streets still hold much of their charm, and open onto some of the most fascinating and picturesque squares in Rome.

DISTANCE: 3.25km (2 miles)
TIME: A half day
START: Piazza Navona
END: Sant'Andrea della Valle
POINTS TO NOTE: The fairly small geographical area covered here is full of restaurants and cafés, making it easy to stop for a break and extend the route to a full day. Consider starting in the early morning if you want to browse the fruit-and-vegetable market at Campo de' Fiori.

The route starts with theatrical fountains on the grand Piazza Navona and continues by exploring the surrounding neighbourhood, eventually arriving at the Campo de' Fiori, known for its exceptional morning market and night-time bars.

PIAZZA NAVONA

The pedestrian **Piazza Navona** ❶ is filled with covered tables, gelaterie, hawkers, street performers, portrait painters, tourists and locals. It is one of the few places where you can spot politicians munching sandwiches next to dog-walking pensioners and wide-eyed tour groups, all in the shadow of a Baroque fountain.

History
The skinny floor plan of the piazza follows the layout of the ancient Stadium of Domitian from the 1st century AD. Domitian's sports stadium predates the construction of the Colosseum and was used for races and other 'agone' or games. The seating could hold over 30,000 spectators, and the stadium was in use as late as the 5th century. The current piazza echoes the seating area in the curve of the surrounding buildings.

The fountains
The bold look of the piazza dates to the 17th century with the patronage of Pope Innocent X Pamphilj. Gianlorenzo Bernini started the fountain project in 1648 after weighting the open competition for the commis-

Street performers   Fountain of the Moor

sion in his favour. His magnificent plan for the **Fontana dei Quattro Fiumi** (Fountain of the Four Rivers) incorporated the obelisk from the Circus of Maxentius. Four continental rivers are represented by massive allegorical figures, providing a connection between the powers of the waters and the powers of the continents. Depicted are the Danube for Europe, the Ganges for Asia, the Nile for Africa and La Plata for America. The figures provide architectural supports to lift the massive obelisk above the waterfalls. Integrated in the composition is the papal insignia of Innocent X.

The two other fountains predate Bernini's centrepiece. These works are primarily by Giacomo della Porta from the late 1570s. The **Fontana di Nettuno** (Fountain of Neptune) is located at the north end, and the **Fontana del Moro** (Fountain of the Moor) at the south.

Sant'Agnese in Agone
Directly facing the Fontana dei Quattro Fiumi is the church of **Sant' Agnese in Agone ❷** (Saint Agnes in Navona; Tue–Fri 9am–1pm,

3pm–7pm and Sat–Sun 9am–1pm, 4pm–8pm; Services on Sat at 7pm, Sun 12.15pm and 7pm), distinguished by its rolling concave facade. The exterior appearance of the church is the work of Bernini's rival Francesco Borromini. The church is dedicated to St Agnes, an early martyr who was publicly executed in the Stadium of Domitian in 304 AD. The Baroque interior of the space is stunning, and the high-relief side altars complement the massive sculptural centrepiece depicting the Miracle of Sant'Agnese.

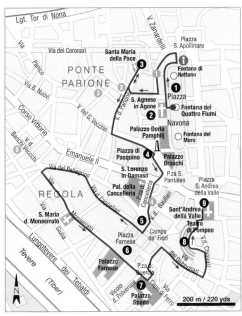

Campo de' Fiori

Palazzo Pamphilj

Before leaving Piazza Navona, have a look at the long palace at the left of the church. The **Palazzo Pamphilj** (not to be confused with the nearby Galleria Doria Pamphilj, see page 48) was once home to Pope Innocent X and, like the piazza in front, was decorated accordingly. It is now the seat of the Brazilian Embassy, but some of the great frescoes by Pietro da Cortona can be seen through the massive windows that look onto the piazza. It is tempting to stop for a meal on the Piazza Navona but much of the food is overpriced.

Exit the piazza at the north end, past the Fontana di Nettuno, and turn left on the Piazza Sant'Apollinare. Directly on the left you will find a small open archaeological area. Some of the entry arches and concession shops of the Stadium of Domitian are visible. Continue bearing left, past the triangular-shaped Largo Febo, which becomes Via Santa Maria del Anima.

At the corner is **Osteria dell Anima**, see ❶. The outdoor tables and a non-stop kitchen make it a failsafe lunch or dinner spot.

If you prefer a short break at one of the cool retro cafés then continue along to Via di Tor Millina and right to the Via della Pace. For a quick coffee or a trendy aperitivo, head to the popular **Bar del Fico**, see ❷, just around the corner.

SANTA MARIA DELLA PACE

Tucked into the end of the street, just past the Antico Caffè della Pace, is the little church of **Santa Maria della Pace** ❸ (Vicolo dell'Arco della Pace 5; Mon, Wed and Sat 9–midday; charge for concerts). The church, dedicated to St Mary of Peace, was started under Pope Sixtus IV in honour of a peace agreement forged with Turkey in 1482. Much of the space was remodelled by Pietro da Cortona. There are frescoes by Raphael, Rosso Fiorentino and Baldassarre Peruzzi. Perhaps the most important space is the Bramante cloister (now a space for art exhibitions), which was commissioned in 1504 by Cardinal Carafa. Donato Bramante eventually worked on the grand plan for the construction of St Peter's.

Street of the old government

Facing away from Santa Maria della Pace, head south along the Via di Parione to the Via del Governo Vecchio (street of the old government). This lovely cobbled lane is chock-full of boutiques, vintage shops, bijou jewellery stores and clubs. The best pizzeria in Rome – **Da Baffetto**, see ❸ – is located just up the street to the right.

To continue, turn left onto the Via del Governo Vecchio and head to the small triangular-shaped Piazza di Pasquino.

PIAZZA DI PASQUINO

This piazza-turned-car park is home to one of Rome's legendary characters, **Pasquino** ❹, whose statue stands on

Santa Maria della Pace

Food market on Campo de' Fiori

a pedestal at one end of the piazza. The statue was placed on display in 1501 by Cardinal Carafa, where it quickly assumed the role of 'talking statue' (see page 13). For the past five hundred years Pasquino has acted as a kind of outlet for public expression. Political satire or notes against papal policy are posted anonymously and can still be found on the front of the plinth. Pasquino's commentary is still occasionally quoted in the daily newspapers.

CAMPO DE' FIORI

Continue south on Via di San Pantaleo and cross the busy Corso Vittorio Emanuele II onto the Piazza della Cancelleria (Papal Chancellery). Just off this street is another excellent restaurant option at **Ditirambo**, see ❹.

History of the piazza

Past the Palazzo della Cancelleria is the piazza of the **Campo de' Fiori** ❺ (Field of Flowers). The 'campo' has really been the centre of Roman life since at least the 15th century. At one point it was a simple flower field, but over the years it has been a meat market, a site for public execution and political rallies, a fruit and flower market, and home to numerous bars and restaurants. It can be said that this is the only true square in the city, in that it is the one piazza not attached to a temple or church.

During the medieval period the piazza was the main market and focal point for the influx of pilgrims. Many of the street names in the surrounding area still reflect their medieval use. Via dei Balestrari was where crossbow makers worked, Via dei Cappellari was for hat-makers and Via dei Chiavari was dedicated to locksmiths. The current look of the piazza is related to urban planning in the 15th century after the return of the papacy from France, an event that dramatically changed the city. In the middle of the piazza is a statue commemorating the philosopher Giordano Bruno, who was burnt at the stake in Campo de' Fiori in 1600. Bruno was found guilty of heresy for believing that the earth was not the centre of the universe. The philosopher was the originator of the concept of 'free thought'.

The piazza today

Today the busy Campo de' Fiori continues to be a hub of sorts. A wonderful fruit-and-vegetable market still sets up each morning at dawn (Mon–Sat). By lunchtime (around 2pm), when the market closes for the day, groups of local businessmen and women can be seen eating on the square. In the evenings strolling families fill the piazza, and by nightfall the restaurants and bars are crammed with university students.

The neighbourhood

Taking the Via dei Capellari, from the west side of the piazza, leads you

Huge basin on Piazza Farnese

into the surrounding medieval quarter. Continue to the Via del Pellegrino (the Pilgrims' Way), which, as the name suggests, was constructed to deal with the flow of traffic for pilgrims visiting St Peter's. Keeping left brings you to a small piazza. Make a sharp left turn onto the Via Monserrato, the more elegant of the medieval streets.

Nearby, on the Via dei Banchi Vecchi is **Il Goccetto**, see ⑤, a little wine bar.

Continue southeast on Via Monserrato to Piazza Farnese. Though it actually adjoins the Campo de' Fiori, this piazza feels worlds apart.

PIAZZA FARNESE

The focal point of the **Piazza Farnese** ⑥ is the **Palazzo Farnese** (closed to the public), considered the finest of the Renaissance palaces. The palazzo was begun for Pope Paul III while he was still Cardinal Farnese. Work started in 1514 by Antonio da Sangallo, and was passed along to Michelangelo who added the upper floors and the finely ordered decoration. The two massive basins in the piazza were taken from the Baths of Caracalla (see page 37). Palazzo Farnese is now home to the French Embassy.

PALAZZO SPADA

One street off the Piazza Farnese, on the Via Capo di Ferro, sits the small

Palazzo Spada ⑦ (Piazza Capo di Ferro 13; http://galleriaspada.beni-culturali.it; daily 8.30am–7.30pm). This ingenious palazzo is recognizable by its stuccoed facade of the 1540s. Borromini was commissioned to modify the space, and he added a trompe l'oeil (fool the eye) masterpiece of false perspective. In order to create the look of a non-existent garden, he constructed a tiny colonnade that creates the perception of a large garden portico. Part of the palace now houses offices of the High Court, and the public galleries display Cardinal Spada's exceptional art collection. Exhibits are unmarked works by Titian, Guercino, Rubens, Caravaggio, Domenichino, Parmigianino, as well as Andrea del Sarto, and both Orazio and Artemisia Gentileschi.

THEATRE OF POMPEY

Take the Via dei Balestrari to the edge of the Campo de' Fiori, and turn right, heading east into the pedestrian shopping street of Via dei Giubbonari. Turn left on Via dei Chiavari; at the first left is a small street with tall buildings following the curve of the **Teatro di Pompeo** ⑧ (Theatre of Pompey). The original theatre was built in 55 BC, and was not only the world's largest theatre but also the first permanent one. It was here, in the attached Curia Pompeia, that Julius Caesar was stabbed to death in 44 BC.

Palazzo Spada   *Palazzo Farnese*

SANT'ANDREA DELLA VALLE

At the end of the street, facing the traffic of the Corso Vittorio Emanuele II, is the church of **Sant'Andrea della Valle** ❾ (Piazza Sant'Andrea della Valle; 7.30am–12.30pm, 4.30–7.30pm). This large structure sits directly on the busy Corso, making it difficult to appreciate the size of the church and dome. Construction was carried out in two phases and completed by Carlo Maderno in 1625. The massive dome and windows make this one of the best naturally lit churches in the city. The interior decoration is in keeping with the high Baroque style, and the swirling ceiling frescoes depicting the *Glory of Paradise* by Giovanni Lanfranco are a prime example of the tastes of the period. There are often summer and evening concerts performed here – check at the entrance for the concert schedule.

Food and drink

❶ OSTERIA DELL ANIMA

Via Santa Maria dell'Anima 8; tel: 06-686 4661; www.osteriadellanima.com; noon–midnight; €€

This osteria has indoor and outdoor seating and an extensive menu. The signature pear-filled *fiocchetti* pasta in a carrot and pear cream is delicious, as are the fish dishes.

❷ BAR DEL FICO

Piazza del Fico, 26; tel: 06-6889 1373; daily 7am–2am; €

This historic bar caters to the local population in the morning and to a varied and trendy crowd in the evening. Breakfast is relaxed, lunch simple but delightfully fresh, and the evening cocktails are to die for.

❸ DA BAFFETTO

Via del Governo Vecchio 114; tel: 06-686 1617; www.pizzeriabaffetto.it; noon–3pm, 6.30pm–1am; €

Stop in for a legendary thin-crust pizza. Baffetto gets packed out, so be prepared to wait in the queue for a table. Excellent.

❹ DITIRAMBO

Piazza della Cancelleria 74; tel: 06-687 1626; www.ristoranteditirambo.it; Mon 7–11pm, Tue–Sun 12.45–3.15pm, 7–11.30pm;
€€

This is a fail-safe choice for an excellent (largely organic) dinner, at a fair price, in a good location. They have seasonal dishes including bean soup, plus specialities like ravioli with pumpkin sauce. Reserve.

❺ IL GOCCETTO

Via dei Banchi Vecchi 14; tel: 06-686 4268; Tue–Sat noon–midnight, Mon 6.30pm–midnight; €€

This traditional yet relaxed pre-dinner wine bar serves some fantastic wines by the glass. The cheese plates or salmon rolls are a perfect addition to any bottle.

The Ara Pacis

ARA PACIS TO THE PANTHEON

Tucked away in a relatively small area of the centre are some of the most inspiring monuments in Rome. This route covers the emblematic Ara Pacis, the elegance of the Galleria Pamphilj and the wonder of the Pantheon.

DISTANCE: 2km (1.25 miles)
TIME: A half day
START: Ara Pacis
END: Piazza della Rotonda
POINTS TO NOTE: This is a great walk for morning or afternoon. There is a lot to take in but the route is contained in a fairly small geographical area and there are plenty of opportunities for coffee or ice cream breaks. Children generally like this route.

Start the route on the Via di Ripetta, located just south of the Piazza del Popolo and a few minutes' stroll west of the Spanish Steps.

ARA PACIS

The **Museo dell'Ara Pacis** ❶ (Ara Pacis Museum; Lungotevere in Augusta; www.arapacis.it; 9.30am–7.30pm) is a dazzling contemporary white structure designed by Richard Meier to house the Ara Pacis Augustae (Altar of Majes-

tic Peace), one of the best examples of early Roman sculpture.

The focal point of the museum is the grand altar; what we see today are the remaining sections of a large sacrificial altar used for public ceremony and offerings of peace. The altar was consecrated in 9 BC under Emperor Augustus to celebrate his war victories in Gaul and Hispania, and became the most important symbol of the Pax Romana, a time of peace and prosperity from 27 BC to 180 AD. The beautiful and unusually life-like relief carvings depict Augustus and his family in the sacrificial processional of 13 BC.

MAUSOLEUM OF AUGUSTUS

Next to the Ara Pacis is the overgrown **Mausoleo di Augusto** ❷, located in the piazza. This now dilapidated ruin would have been finished with carved marble decorations and statuary. The circular building was built in 28 BC as a family mausoleum, and the funerary urns of the Emperors Tiberius, Caligula and Claudius were also placed here.

Great flavours at Giolitti

Relief carving on the Ara Pacis

The entrance was marked with Egyptian obelisks, which now stand in the Piazza del Quirinale (see page 54) and at Santa Maria Maggiore (see page 83).

On two sides of the piazza is a Fascist-era colonnade, home to some great eateries. Try **Gusto al 28**, see ❶, where the outdoor seating extends under the covered portico.

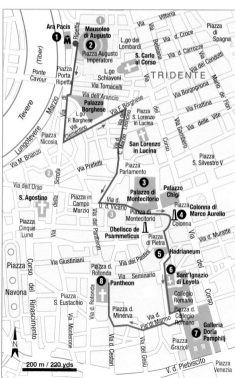

REFRESHMENTS

Nearby are two good options for refreshment. Exit the Piazza Augusto Imperatore at the southwest corner, where Via di Ripetta becomes Via della Scrofa. At No. 104 is **Alfredo's**, see ❷. Alternatively, from Piazza Nicosia, turn left onto Via del Clementino, continue past Piazza Borghese, and turn right at Via del Leoncino. A short way along is a fine piazza named after the 12th-century church of **San Lorenzo in Lucina**. Continue south along the shopping street of Via di Campo Marzio until you come to Via degli Ufficio del Vicario, where you will see **Giolitti**, see ❸, one of the best gelato spots in the city. They have been perfecting their family recipe since 1870.

GOVERNMENT BUILDINGS

Continue to the end of the street to Piazza di Montecitorio, named after the fortress-like **Palazzo di Montecitorio** ❸, designed by Gianlorenzo Bernini in the 1620s. Nowadays, the palace is the seat

Inside the Pantheon

of the Italian Chamber of Deputies (Houses of Parliament). In front is the **Obelisco de Psammetichus**, an Egyptian obelisk dating from the 10th century BC. Its shadow indicated the time on the sundial of the Ara Pacis.

Piazza Colonna
At the far side the piazza opens onto the front of the adjoining **Palazzo Chigi**, official residence of the prime minister. The square in front of the palazzo is known as the **Piazza Colonna**, after the **Colonna di Marco Aurelio ❹** (Column of Marcus Aurelius) in the centre.

This 30m (100ft) -high column is a triumphal monument depicting the war victories of the Emperor Marcus Aurelius in 176 AD. It is made in the style of Trajan's Column, and carved out of 28 fitted blocks of Carrara marble. The relief carving flows in a continual spiral from the ground upwards, revealing all of the battle details in chronological order.

Just south of the Piazza Colonna is the Piazza di Pietra with the remnants (11 fluted Corinthian columns) of the 2nd-century **Hadrianeum ❺** (Temple of Hadrian), encased in what is now part of the stock exchange.

SANT' IGNAZIO DI LOYOLA

Continuing south along the tiny Via de' Burro is the Baroque wonder of **Sant'Ignazio di Loyola ❻** (Piazza di Sant'Ignazio; Mon–Sat 7.30am–7pm, Sun 9am–7pm). Built in 1626, it is most

famous for its Baroque interior and masterpieces of decorative illusion. The nave ceiling is covered with the bright frescoes by Andrea Pozzo, who used *trompe l'oeil* to create three-dimensional space. Further along the nave is a spot on the floor marking the ideal vantage point to see the dome. Look carefully, as this is also a trick of the artist. The dome is false, having been painted on a flat surface.

GALLERIA DORIA PAMPHILJ

At the back of the church, along the Via Sant'Ignazio, is the parking area of the Piazza del Collegio Romano and the entrance to the **Galleria Doria Pamphilj ❼** (Via del Corso 305; daily 9am–7pm, last entry at 6pm). The palace is still inhabited by the Pamphilj family, who own one of the best private art collections in Italy. The collection was started by Pope Innocent X Pamphilj and now includes over four hundred paintings. Highlights include art by Titian, Raphael, Brueghel, Ribera, and Parmigianino. Of note are rare early works by Caravaggio, such as the *Penitent Magdalene*, and the powerful *Portrait of Pope Innocent X* by Velázquez displayed next to the *Bust of Pope Innocent X* by Bernini.

THE PANTHEON

Continue the route by walking west from the Piazza del Collegio Romano along the Via del Pie' di Marmo to the Piazza della Minerva, noted for the elephant

Link to the heavens   *Piazza della Rotonda*

statue by Bernini. Head around to the front of the **Pantheon** ❽, also known as the Basilica di Santa Maria ad Martyres (Piazza della Rotonda; Mon–Sat 8.30am–7.30pm, Sun 9am–6pm). The present structure has been in use since it was built in 125 AD under the Emperor Hadrian. It was designed as a temple to the 12 most important Classical gods. In 608, under the Emperor Phocas, the Pantheon was converted from a pagan temple to the church of St Mary of the Martyrs. This act likely saved it from complete destruction.

Interior

The impact of walking through the original bronze doors into the Pantheon is staggering. The height and diameter of the coffered dome are exactly the same measurement (43.3m/142ft), meaning that the space inside creates a perfect sphere, the symbol of spiritual perfection. Light enters through the open oculus above, a circular hole measuring 9m (30ft) in diameter, symbolically linking the temple and the heavens on high. The coffered part of the dome was built out of poured concrete that progressively thins near the top edge. The walls are 6m (20ft) thick at their base to support the weight of the massive structure. Much of the interior marble decoration and flooring is original, but there have been additions and modifications. The tomb of Raphael can be found to the left of the main altar, opposite that of King Vittorio Emanuele I.

Piazza della Rotonda

In front of the Pantheon is the Piazza della Rotonda. In the centre is a fountain with steps supporting a small but elegant obelisk from the Temple of Isis.

Food and drink

❶ GUSTO AL 28

Piazza Augusto Imperatore 9; tel: 06-6813 4221; www.gusto.it; 8am–late; € café/€€€ restaurant

This fun multiplex of dining offers something for everyone. The pizzeria and the outdoor café and bar are the most economical options, while the osteria and restaurant are pricier, but offer an extended menu to match.

❷ ALFREDO ALLA SCROFA

Via della Scrofa 104; tel: 06-6880 6163; www.alfredoallascrofa.com; daily 12.30–3pm, 6–11pm; €€€

The traditional Roman feel and great food keep this place popular. Specialities include fettuccine Alfredo, risotto, pasta with seafood, and the house white truffle sauce.

❸ GIOLITTI

Via degli Uffici del Vicario 40; tel: 06-699 1243; www.giolitti.it; daily 7am–1am; €

This famous historic gelateria serves wonderful handmade ice cream in flavours including cinnamon, and watermelon with chocolate seeds. They also serve coffee, cakes and sandwiches.

Taking a break on the Spanish Steps

SPANISH STEPS, TRIDENTE AND TREVI FOUNTAIN

This route covers Rome's fashionable shopping district. The grand Spanish Steps give way to the Via dei Condotti, one of the most exclusive and understated retail addresses in the world. Not far away is the iconic Trevi Fountain.

DISTANCE: 2.5km (1.5 miles)
TIME: A half day
START: Piazza di Spagna
END: Trevi Fountain
POINTS TO NOTE: Consider either starting quite early in the morning or in the cool of the late afternoon. Many of the shops on this route stay open in the summer until 8pm.

The route begins at the Piazza di Spagna (metro line A, Spagna), a lively space that could be called the city centre. The piazza has been Rome's most popular meeting point for centuries.

PIAZZA DI SPAGNA

At the centre of the **Piazza di Spagna 1** is the early Baroque fountain called **Fontana della Barcaccia** (Fountain of the Ugly Boat). The basin looks like an ancient sailing vessel and was designed in 1625 by Pietro Bernini, father to the more famous Gianlorenzo. It has supplied clean drinking water and been a focal point to the piazza for generations. Leading away from the piazza is the elegant Via dei Condotti, with designer shops cornering the square.

Spanish Steps

Straight up from the piazza are the picture-perfect **Scalinata di Trinità dei Monti** or **Spanish Steps 2**, built in 1725. On the right corner as you look up is the house where John Keats lived until his death in 1821. His friend Percy Shelley wrote the poem *Mourn not for Adonis* in honour of the sombre occasion; Shelley drowned the following year. Both writers are buried in Rome's Protestant Cemetery (see page 79), and the house on the Spanish Steps has been turned into the **Keats-Shelley Memorial House 3** (Piazza di Spagna 26; www.keats-shelley-house.org; Mon–Sat 10am–1pm, 2–6pm). The small museum displays memorabilia.

Opposite, to the left of the steps, are the tearooms at **Babington's**, see 1, which have been serving travellers, including English ones, since 1893.

Fontana della Barcaccia   *Via dei Condotti high-end shopping*

Trinità dei Monti

At the top of the 137 steps is the crowning terrace and the Egyptian obelisk found in the Gardens of Sallust. Above is the elegant facade of the church of **Trinità dei Monti** ❹ (Piazza Trinità dei Monti; Tue–Sun 6.30am–8pm, Thu 6.30am–12pm), with matching bell-towers creating the architectural symmetry. The church was constructed in 1502 under the patronage of the French King Louis XII. Inside is a colourful fresco series by Taddeo Zuccari and two paintings by Daniele da Volterra, Michelangelo's student and assistant.

Villa Medici

To the left of the church, along the Viale Trinità dei Monti, is the Tuscan inspired **Villa Medici**, which now houses the **Accademia di Francia** ❺ (French Academy; www.villamedici.it; ticket office open Tue–Sun 9.30am–5.30pm, until 6.30pm if there is an exhibition). The villa was once owned by Cardinal Ferdinando I de' Medici, Grand Duke of Tuscany, who amassed a great art collection to rival that of the Borghese nearby. The building was later taken over by the French Academy, which was founded in 1666 by Louis XIV for the education of painters in Rome.

Both Poussin and Ingres were directors, and famous students included Fragonard, Boucher and Debussy. The handsome **Villa Medici gardens** (same as the villa; ticket to villa includes the gardens and temporary exhibitions) were once described by American writer Henry James as 'the most enchanting' place in Rome.

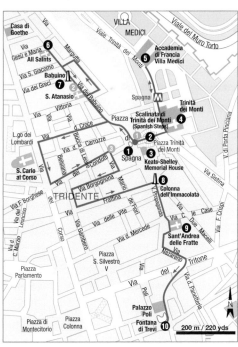

Via Margutta

TRIDENTE

Return to Piazza di Spagna, and head northwest along the Via del Babuino, turn right onto Via degli Orti d'Alibert, and left onto the **Via Margutta**. This hidden street still exudes the charm of the 1960s cinema world, made famous by directors such as Federico Fellini. Browse the interesting shops and galleries, and turn left at the Via dell' Orto di Napoli to re-join the Via del Babuino.

Via del Babuino

To the right of the intersection is the neo-Gothic Anglican church of **All Saints** ❻ (Via del Babuino 153; www. allsaintsrome.org; daily 9am–5pm, Sun services at 8.30am and 10.30am).

The church is on the **Via del Babuino**, one of the three major shopping streets that make up the elegant area called Tridente. The other two are Via del Corso and Via di Ripetta, and they all radiate out from the Piazza del Popolo like prongs of a fork. The Via del Babuino was once home to artists' studios and workshops, and now houses antiques dealers and designers. Walking along the street back towards the Spanish Steps you will see the reclining statue of **Babuino** ❼, the baboon-like character who lends his name to the street. Between the statue and the Greek national church of Sant'Atanasio is the artist's studio that once belonged to sculptor Antonio Canova and his assistant Adamo Tadolini. The space is now an interesting café-museum, the **Café Atelier Canova-Tadolini**, see ❷.

Via del Corso and Via dei Condotti

Turn right at the Via della Croce into the smaller shopping streets between the Tridente. Turn south onto the **Via del Corso**, the longest and straightest of the roads, and considered the city's only high-street shopping district. Turn left again onto the **Via dei Condotti** (now facing the full view of the Spanish Steps at the end of the street). Just past the Via Marlo de' Fiori is the coffee house of coffee houses – the **Antico Caffè Greco**, see ❸.

Colonna dell'Immacolata

From the Caffè Greco, retrace your steps, heading south on the Via Mario de' Fiori. Now turn right onto elegant Via Borgognona, then left onto Via Belsi-

---

Sea god

The focus of Nicola Salvi's Trevi Fountain design is the powerful sea god Neptune. Each of Neptune's Tritons have seahorse chargers, one with an unruly horse representing the oceans or stormy weather, the other with a docile horse representing lakes or still waters. The arrival of the water itself is being heralded by blasts from conch shell horns. At the sides of the main scene are allegorical statues representing health (right) and abundance (left), symbols of the properties of water. A marble relief shows Agrippa commissioning the aqueduct in 19 BC.

| Trevi Fountain | Looking down from the Spanish Steps |

ana, then left again, heading east along the shopping haven of Via Frattina.

At the far end, in the piazza, is the **Colonna dell'Immacolata** ❽, a large column topped by a statue of the Virgin Mary. The erection of the column in 1857 required the assistance of 220 members of the Fire Brigade, who now consider this monument their protector.

Sant'Andrea delle Fratte

Take the Via Propaganda to the church of **Sant'Andrea delle Fratte** ❾ (Via di Sant'Andrea delle Fratte 1; July–Sep daily 6.30am–12.30pm and 4.30–8pm, Oct–June daily 6.30am–1pm and 4–7pm), one of the great remodelling efforts of Francesco Borromini from the 1670s. The dome frescoes by Pasquale Marini and the oversized angel statues by Bernini are particularly lovely.

TREVI FOUNTAIN

Continue along, taking the Via Nazareno and crossing over the busy Via del Tritone onto the Via della Stamperia. The sound of water is audible before the immense **Fontana di Trevi** ❿ comes into view.

The fountain, depicting the sea god Neptune, was completed in 1762, making it a relative newcomer to the urban landscape. The theme celebrates the flow of fresh water into the city, and the name Trevi (tre vie) alludes to the juncture of three 'roads' of water, this being the meeting of the Aqua Vergine, the Aqua Virgo and one of the repaired ancient aqueducts. Popular tradition holds that if you throw a coin in, you will return to Rome. Facing away from the fountain, hold the coin in your right hand, and toss it over your left shoulder.

Food and drink

❶ BABINGTON'S TEA ROOMS
Piazza di Spagna 23; tel: 06-678 6027; www.babingtons.com; daily 10am–9.15pm; €€
These pleasant tearooms have an old world charm. Perfect for afternoon tea, but also suitable for a light lunch or a bacon and egg breakfast.

❷ CAFÉ ATELIER CANOVA-TADOLINI
Via del Babuino 150; tel: 06-3211 0702; www.canovatadolini.com; Mon–Sat 8am–midnight; €€
This lovely museum with a café attached serves excellent cappuccinos, pastas, salads and seasonal dishes at tables dotted among the artworks.

❸ ANTICO CAFFÈ GRECO
Via dei Condotti 86; tel: 06-679 1700; www.anticocaffegreco.eu; daily 9am–9pm; €
This café has been serving the world's intellectuals since 1760. Customers such as Keats, Goethe, Liszt, Casanova, Buffalo Bill, and King Ludwig have found comfort in the velvet sofas and intimate salons. Usually packed with tourists but worth a visit nonetheless.

San Carlo alle Quattro Fontane

QUIRINALE, BARBERINI AND VIA VENETO

Taking in the palaces of the President of the Republic, past Baroque monuments and the rarefied air of the Via Veneto, this route includes some of the glamour spots of the city centre.

DISTANCE: 2km (1.25 miles)
TIME: A half day
START: Piazza del Quirinale
END: Via Veneto at Porta Pinciana
POINTS TO NOTE: If you follow this route in the morning, you could stop for lunch at the top of the Via Veneto, or go for a picnic in Villa Borghese, and continue to route 7 for a full-day itinerary.

This route begins at the piazza in front of the Palazzo del Quirinale, a few minutes southeast of the Trevi Fountain and just up from the Via Nazionale.

QUIRINALE

The panoramic **Piazza del Quirinale** is the entrance to the **Palazzo del Quirinale ❶** (www.quirinale.it; Tue–Wed and Fri–Sun 9.30am–4pm, booking required). This secured complex was originally built over the ruins of the Baths of Constantine. The Renaissance buildings were constructed as the papal summer palaces, and were later used by the king after Unification in the 1870s. It now serves as the official residence of the President of the Italian Republic. The splendid interior is worth a visit.

The focal point of the piazza is the fountain with statues of the twin *Dioscuri* (horse tamers) Castor and Pollux, found in the excavation of the Baths of Constantine, now crowned by an Egyptian obelisk that stood at the Mausoleum of Emperor Augustus (see page 46).

Scuderie del Quirinale

At the corner of the piazza is the **Scuderie del Quirinale ❷** (Quirinale stables; Via XXIV Maggio; www.scuderiequirinale.it; Sun–Thu 10am–8pm, Fri–Sat 10am–10.30pm), built in 1732 as a stables (used until 1932) and now a museum and temporary exhibition space.

Sant'Andrea al Quirinale

Along the Via del Quirinale is Gianlorenzo Bernini's church of **Sant'Andrea al Quirinale ❸** (Via del Quirinale 30; Tue–

Sant'Andrea al Quirinale   *Guard, Palazzo del Quirinale*

Sun 9am–noon, 3–6pm, Sunday Mass at 10.30am), known as the 'pearl of the Baroque'. Though Sant'Andrea is not as grand as the piazza of St Peter's, Bernini considered it his best architectural achievement.

Four fountains

The church is nicely contrasted with that of **San Carlo alle Quattro Fontane** ❹ (Via del Quirinale 23; www.sancarlino.eu; Mon–Fri 10am–1pm, 3–6pm, Sat 10am–1pm, Sun noon–1pm, open for exhibitions only), designed in 1667 by Bernini's rival Francesco Borromini and located further along the Via del Quirinale past a pleasant shady park. The real measurements of the tiny building are ingeniously disguised through Borromini's signature curving, airy design.

At the street junction is the unusual monument of **Le Quattro Fontane** (Four Fountains), mounted on the corners of the buildings facing the intersection. The allegorical figures were designed by Domenico Fontana and represent the *Tiber*,

the *Arno*, *Fidelity* and *Strength*. The Baroque fountain was constructed as part of the urban redevelopment plan of the 1580s under Pope Sixtus V. The street was then called the Via Felice (Street of Happiness) as it connects the churches of Trinità dei Monti, above the Spanish Steps, with Santa Maria Mag-

Palazzo Barberini fresco

giore. The obelisks marking each of these churches can be seen from the crossing.

PALAZZO BARBERINI

Along the Via delle Quattro Fontane is the entrance to one of Rome's best art museums, located inside the **Palazzo Barberini**, now the **Galleria Nazionale d'Arte Antica** ❺ (Via dell Quattro Fontane 13; http://galleriabarberini.benic ulturali.it; Tue–Sun 8am–7pm).

Pope Urban VIII Barberini commissioned some of the top 17th-century architects for the construction of his family palace. The rooms and rich decoration display the tastes of one of the city's most powerful popes; the Barberini inhabited the upper floors until the 1960s.

Highlights are a series of grand halls and Rococo apartments, and a fresco series by Pietro da Cortona depicting the **Triumph of Divine Providence**, which artfully alludes to the papacy of Urban VIII. Paintings in the galleries include works by El Greco, Caravaggio, Guido Reni, Tintoretto, a formal portrait of King Henry VIII by Holbein, and the seductive *La Fornarina* (the little baker) by Raphael. The national art collection is divided with the Palazzo Corsini (see page 70).

Piazza Barberini

In the nearby **Piazza Barberini**, at the centre of the clogged intersec-

tion where seven streets converge, you will discover the playful **Fontana del Tritone**. The leaping dolphins and muscular Triton with serpent legs were designed by Bernini in 1642 to promote the career of Urban VIII. The papal tiara, keys of St Peter, and the heraldic bee emblems of the Barberini family are integrated into the composition. Across the square is the smaller **Fontana delle Api** (Fountain of the Bees) from 1641.

If you are in need of refreshment, try the stylish **Pepy's Bar**, see ❶, located at the southwest corner of the piazza by Via delle Quatro Fontane.

VIA VENETO

At the northern side of the piazza is the start of the **Via Vittorio Veneto** of *La Dolce Vita* fame. The curving tree-lined street has had its fair share of celebrity, but now carries a sense of nostalgia. The trendy cafés and restaurants caught by the flash of the 1960s paparazzi have been replaced with pricey brasseries, embassies and some of Rome's most luxurious hotels. The best choice for lounging in a sophisticated atmosphere that combines the Dolce Vita's retro feel with modern cuisine and decor is **Doney**, see ❷, great for drinks or a meal.

Santa Teresa

Head east along Via Barberini; on the corner of Piazza San Bernardo and

Palazzo Barberini   *Santa Maria della Concezione*

Via XX Settembre stands the church of **Santa Maria della Vittoria**. It contains Bernini's famous Baroque Cornaro chapel, which uses natural light to highlight the *Ecstasy of St Teresa*.

Santa Maria della Concezione

Just up from the Piazza Barberini is the peculiar **Capuchin Crypt and Museum,** located at the church of **Santa Maria della Concezione ❻** (Via Vittorio Veneto 27; daily 9am–6.30pm). Here the skeletal remains of more than 4,000 Capuchin monks are arranged in artistic patterns. If the bones themselves are not sombre enough, the sign at the entrance reads 'What you are now, we once were. What we are now, you shall someday become'.

For something lighter have a look at the paintings by Guido Reni and Pietro da Cortona in the main church.

Porta Pinciana

Continue the walk up the meandering Via Veneto, past shops, the regal Westin Excelsior Hotel at No. 125 and the Palazzo Margherita (now the American Embassy), to end at the **Porta Pinciana**, one of the gateways into the park of the Villa Borghese.

The Porta Pinciana is one of the ancient entries into the city through the Aurelian Walls, which were originally built in 275 under the Emperor Aurelian. The walls once enclosed all seven hills of Rome, although now only a few of the sections remain.

Located just off the Via Veneto is one of Rome's traditional cafés, **Lotti**, see ❸, a family-run business that dates back to 1917.

Food and drink

❶ PEPY'S BAR

Piazza Barberini 56; tel: 06-4040 2364; www.pepysbar.it; daily 7am–2am; €€
This lively locale does great cappuccinos and is also perfect for people-watching over a cocktail. Also does snacks and more substantial meals.

❷ DONEY

Via Vittorio Veneto 125; tel: 06-4708 2783; www.restaurantdoney.com; daily 12.30–10.30pm, Mon–Fri 7–10.30am, Sun brunch 12.30–3pm; €€€
This café has been a hotspot for beautiful people since the 1950s. It is worth a stop for nibbles or an indulgent drink in the café, which combines the retro feel with modern decor, but the restaurant is on the expensive side. Sunday brunch is an excellent choice.

❸ LOTTI

Via Sardegna 19; tel: 06-482 1902; Sun–Fri 6.30am–9.30pm; €
This family-run place is a classic for perfect coffee, homemade pastries, ice creams and great lunch.

Feeding the ducks, Villa Borghese

VILLA BORGHESE TO PIAZZA DEL POPOLO

This route meanders through the most-loved green space in Rome, complete with views, lakes and one of the world's finest private art collections, finishing with a look at the church of Santa Maria del Popolo.

DISTANCE: 3.5km (2 miles)
TIME: A half day
START: Porta Pinciana
END: Piazza del Popolo
POINTS TO NOTE: Advanced booking is essential for the Galleria Borghese. With a morning entry consider a picnic in the park afterwards. Alternatively, do the route in the morning, and book the museum for the afternoon. This is a great route for families with children.

Start at the **Porta Pinciana ❶**, located at the top of the Via Veneto. Alternatively, the park can be reached from Metro A Spagna through the pedestrian tunnel (due to a series of escalator accidents in 2018 some stations are sporadically closed for repairs). Taxis are the simplest option for getting to the Galleria Borghese directly.

VILLA BORGHESE

The park of the **Villa Borghese** is the most popular outdoor area, and, at 80 hectares (200 acres), the second largest park, in the city. This green space, with museums, lakes, a horse track, theatres, jogging routes, tennis, temples, cycling lanes, bike rentals and views, was only opened as a public area in 1903. The grand path of the Viale del Museo Borghese leads from the Porta Pinciana to the Galleria Borghese, a 'country' villa turned museum.

Galleria Borghese

For nearly 300 years the villa belonged to the Borghese family, who used it for entertaining and for the display of their private art collection. Now considered the jewel box of Rome, the **Galleria Borghese ❷** (Piazzale Scipione Borghese 5; http://galleriaborghese.benicul turali.it; Tue–Sun 9am–7pm; booking essential, with entry every two hours) showcases the exceptional collection of Cardinal Scipione Borghese.

The museum is arranged on two levels. The ground floor is home to sculpture and antiquities, with the upper floor showcasing the paintings collection. Ticketing, a cloakroom, bookshop and small café can all be found on the lower ground floor.

Galleria Borghese

Exploring on four wheels

History of the collection

When Pope Paul V Borghese came into power in 1605 he quickly appointed his favourite nephew as cardinal (one of the great cases of nepotism). The young Cardinal Scipione was an avid art collector and set about purchasing properties and building a villa to house his growing collections. Scipione had an eye for combining stunning paintings, juxtaposed with Classical antiquities and complemented with contemporary sculpture, most of which was commissioned for the villa itself. The collections went through two major changes with the addition of thematic ceiling decoration in the 18th century, and the loss of a large amount of artwork to the Louvre in 1809. This 'exchange' was conveniently arranged through Napoleon Bonaparte's sister, Paolina, who was married to Camillo Borghese.

Ground floor

Do not miss the rare 4th-century floor mosaics of gladiators, surrounded by elegant sculptures of Roman gods and busts of emperors on the ground floor. Also here are three of Bernini's most famous works. These early masterpieces from the 1620s were commissioned specifically for the villa and include the brooding *David*, the sensuous *Rape of Proserpine*, and the perfect *Apollo and Daphne*, with marble leaves so thinly carved that light shines through them. Other highlights are Antonio Canova's *Venus Victrix*, which portrays Paolina (Bonaparte) Borghese as the half-naked reclining Venus, and five stunning paintings by Caravaggio, including the *Boy with a Basket of Fruit* and the controversial *Palafrenieri Madonna*.

Upper floor

The upper floor, traditionally housing the living quarters, showcases two versions of Bernini's official portrait bust of Cardinal Scipione (he was not happy with the first one). Also on display are some of Raphael's early works such as

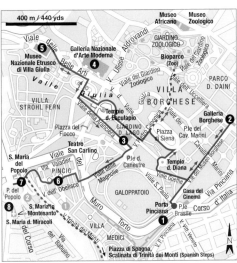

Panoramic Pincio terrace

the brilliant altarpiece from 1507 of the *Deposition of Christ*, Correggio's evocative *Danae*, and Titian's classic *Sacred and Profane Love* from 1514.

Park and lake garden

The vast gardens surrounding the villa are now home to a number of attractions. In addition to the museums there are jogging and bicycle paths, picnic areas and places for outdoor concerts – all under the famous umbrella pines.

Walk back along Viale del Museo Borghese and turn right on Viale Goethe. Here you can hire bikes (Bici Pincio; tel: 06-678 4374; daily 10am–sunset), rent a rikshaw and catch the Trenino (children's train).

Take the Viale della Pineta north past the **Temple of Diana** to the **Piazza di Siena**. If you are lucky your visit here might coincide with a showjumping competition. To the west is the **Giardino del Lago ❸**, with its picturesque lake and floating island temple. There is a small outdoor coffee house nearby and rowing boats for hire.

The zoo (Bioparco)

If you have children, you could make a detour northeast from Piazza di Siena on Via Pietro Canonico; at the north of the park is the **Bioparco** (www. bioparco.it; Apr–Sept 9.30am–7pm, Oct 9.30am–6pm, Nov–Mar 9.30am–5pm). Linked to the zoo is the **Museo Zoologico** (Via Ulisse Aldrovandi 18; http://museo dizoologia.it; Tue–Sun 9am–7pm), which

functions as a natural history collection.

National Gallery of Modern Art

North of the lake, at Viale delle Belle Arti 131, is the **Galleria Nazionale d'Arte Moderna ❹** (www.gnam.beniculturali. it; Tue–Sun 8.30am–7.30pm), featuring art by 19th- and 20th-century Italian painters. The focus is on Romantic landscapes, but there are also works by Courbet, Cezanne, Degas and Monet. The gallery café inside the museum is also worth a visit.

National Etruscan Museum

Continue to the far west of the park, where the **Museo Nazionale Etrusco ❺** (Piazzale di Villa Giulia 9; http://villagiulia. beniculturali.it; Tue–Sun 9am–8pm) is housed in the **Villa Giulia**, former home of Pope Julius III. On display are some of the most important Etruscan pieces in the world. Not to be missed is the repatriated Euphronios Krater, one of the best examples of red-figure Greek pottery in the world, and a 6th-century BC sarcophagus of a married couple sharing a meal into the afterlife.

The Pincio

Return to the National Gallery of Modern Art and head southeast past the lake until you reach Piazzale delle Canestre, where you should turn southwest along Viale delle Magnolie. This leads towards the **Giardini del Pincio ❻** (Pincio Gardens) re-designed by Giuseppe Valadier under Napoleon in 1809. Here

Café Canova   *Obelisk on Piazza del Popolo*

you will find **Casina Valadier**, see ❶.

At the opposite side of Pincio is the **San Carlino puppet theatre** (Viale dei Bambini; www.sancarlino.it; performances Sat, Sun, 10.30am–1.30pm, 2.30pm–5.30pm), hosting traditional Italian shows for children.

The **Pincio terrace** provides romantic views, complete with St Peter's in the distance. Descend by the side stairs to the Piazza del Popolo below. As an alternate ending to the route, take the Via Trinità dei Monti southeast, past the Villa Medici, to the top of the Spanish Steps (see page 50).

PIAZZA DEL POPOLO

The large oval **Piazza del Popolo** ❼ is the hub of Tridente (see page 52). The focal point of this large space is the magnificent Egyptian obelisk from Heliopolis, dating from 1300 BC. Facing into the piazza are the twin churches of **Santa Maria dei Miracoli** and **Santa Maria in Montesanto**, designed by Carlo Rainaldi in the 1660s. On the corner of the piazza at Via del Babuino is the **Canova**, see ❷.

Santa Maria del Popolo

At the north corner of the piazza, near the **Porta Flaminia** (or Porta del Popolo), one of the original gateways into the centre of Rome, is the treasure-filled **Santa Maria del Popolo** ❽ (Mon–Fri 7.30am–12.30pm, 4–7pm, Sat 7.30am–7pm, Sun & holy days 7.30am–1.30pm, 4.30pm–7pm; no vis-

its allowed during Mass). Much of the current church was constructed in 1472 under Pope Sixtus IV (best known for his commission of the Sistine Chapel). It is loaded with Renaissance masterpieces, including the Chigi chapel designed by Raphael, and Pinturicchio frescoes in the Della Rovere chapel. The finest decoration is in the Cerasi chapel where *The Crucifixion of St Peter* and the luminous *Conversion of St Paul* attest to Caravaggio's genius.

Food and drink

❶ CASINA VALADIER

Piazza Bucarest; tel: 06-6992 2090; www.casinavaladier.com; Tue–Sun 12.30–3pm, 7.30–11pm; €€€

The menu is not particularly memorable considering the price, but the view and the service are spectacular. It is a perfect stop for an afternoon tea or drink, or for a romantic meal.

❷ CANOVA

Piazza del Popolo 16; tel: 06-361 2231; http://lnx.canovapiazzadelpopolo.it; daily 7am–11pm; € (café) €€€ (restaurant)

Although the Canova has lost some of its old world charm it still retains some of its former reputation. Fine food is served in the restaurant which has garden seating, while drinks are served in a separate bar. For a snack or drink on the piazza there is the less expensive street-side café service.

Nuns on Piazza San Pietro

THE VATICAN

The Vatican is quintessentially Roman. With over 2,000 years of history, no other place embodies so much politics, history, religion and art all rolled into one relatively small space. Each century has visibly superimposed itself upon the last, forming a great historic layer cake.

DISTANCE: 1.5km (1 mile), not including distance covered in museums
TIME: A full day
START: Piazza San Pietro
END: Vatican Museums
POINTS TO NOTE: The Vatican can be draining with the long queues at security. Pace yourself and bring a bottle of water. Going to the museums in the late morning or early afternoon can reduce the wait. Be sure to dress appropriately (no shorts, sleeveless tops or skirts above the knee).

The start of this route is the huge **Piazza San Pietro ❶** (St Peter's Square). There is time to look around the Basilica of St Peter's, climb the dome, and see Michelangelo's Pietà before walking around the fortified walls of the Vatican Museums and the Sistine Chapel.

VATICAN CITY

The Vatican is one of the most significant tourist sights in the world, with millions of visitors each year. Its role as a political and religious power is unique, and with roughly 1000 inhabitants it is the world's smallest independent state. Vatican City was granted political independence from Italy in 1929, and the Pope is head of both government and state. The Vatican has its own postal system, currency, passport, licence plate, flag and police.

Vatican Hill

Vatican City sits on a large hill. The name comes from the Latin, *Mons Vaticanus* (Vatican Mount) and predates Christianity. The complex of buildings was constructed over a first-century 'circus' built by the Emperor Caligula. The area was expanded by the Emperor Nero, who used it for games and for the persecution of Christians and other non-pagans. It was under Nero that St Peter was martyred in the circus complex. He was buried nearby on the Vatican Hill, and it was this tomb that became the centre of Christianity.

In 326 the Emperor Constantine built the first Christian temple above St Peter's tomb. This became the heart of the Catholic church, and over the

St Peter's   *View from the dome of St Peter's*

centuries the area around the basilica was expanded. The original building was torn down and built anew from the papacy of Julius II in 1506 onwards. What we now call the Vatican is primarily a Renaissance plan.

St Peter's Square

The giant elliptical-shaped piazza was added in 1656 during the final phase of decoration of the new basilica. Bernini was commissioned by Pope Alexander VII to create an architectural space that reflected the role of the church. The floor plan of the piazza is shaped like a giant keyhole, reinforcing the role of St Peter as the gatekeeper to heaven.

The focal point of the piazza is the Egyptian obelisk brought from Alexandria in 37 AD under Emperor Caligula. The fountains are by Maderno and della Fontana, while above Bernini's colonnade are over 200 colossal statues depicting minor saints.

Under the north colonnade is the security checkpoint to St Peter's Basilica. There is often a long queue here but it

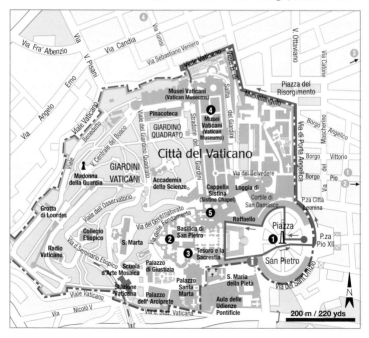

Light streaming into St Peter's

moves quite quickly. A second checkpoint near the steps is for clothing control.

ST PETER'S BASILICA

Construction of the **Basilica di San Pietro** ❷ (Piazza San Pietro; www.vatican.va; 7am – 7pm, until 6pm in winter) was a serious undertaking, with multiple architects, including Bramante, Raphael, Michelangelo (who designed the cupola, or dome) and Maderno, involved. After 120 years, the building was consecrated in 1626.

The Pietà

In the right chapel, protected by thick glass, is the statue of the *Pietà* by Michelangelo. This touching depiction of the death of Christ was completed in 1499 when the artist was only 25.

Down the central nave, past the side chapels, is a lovely 13th-century statue of *St Peter* by Arnolfo di Cambio. This is the official representation of St Peter, and is one of the few works of art that remains from the older structure. His foot has been lovingly kissed and petted for centuries.

Works of art

At the centre is the massive bronze *Baldacchino* hovering over the Papal altar, and marking the tomb of St Peter. This emblematic work by Bernini was commissioned by Pope Urban VIII in 1624, and is the largest freestanding bronze structure in the world. It is dwarfed under Michelangelo's stunning cupola.

Just beyond the altar are more works by Bernini, the *Throne of St Peter in Glory* and window of the *Holy Spirit*. Past the apse, along the left side over a door, is the sombre monument to Pope Alexander VII. This late work by Bernini shows a bronze skeleton as the allegory of death, holding an empty hourglass.

Treasury, grottoes and cupola

There are separate entrances for the additional sites within St Peter's. Entrances to the **Tesoro e Sacrestia** ❸ (Treasury and Sacristy; 9am – 6.15pm, until 5.15pm in winter) are found on the south wall of the nave; the lower-level **grottoes** (7am – 6pm, until 5pm in winter) are situated on the north side of the basilica, accessed from the front portico.

Another rewarding walk is the climb up to the **cupola** (8am – 6pm, until 5pm in winter). Look for the entrance as it is often rerouted for crowd control. There is a lift part way, and then another 320 steps to the top of the spectacular lantern at the top of the dome.

Lunch stop

A break is recommended before continuing to the Vatican Museums, which are about a 15-minute walk around the outside of the Vatican walls. Just a few streets off the Via Porta Angelica the dining options become slightly more tolerable and less of an obvious tourist trap.

If time is short, the **Vatican Museums Café** is an option, or for a more relaxed lunch, you could try **Tre Pupazzi**

Dome of St Peter's   *Close-up of the dome, St Peter's*

on the Borgo Pio, see 1. **Da Benito e Gilberto**, see 2, is good for oysters, while the **Gelateria dei Gracchi** is a short walk away in Prati, see 3.

VATICAN MUSEUMS

Continue along the walls to the entrance of the **Musei Vaticani** 4 (Viale Vaticano 100; www.museivaticani.va; Mon–Sat 9am–6pm, last entry 4pm, see website for exceptions and advanced ticketing; free last Sun of month, not including Easter Sunday, with entry hours 9am–12.30pm). At the entry is another security check-point, and ticketing is located on the first floor. Maps with suggested routes are available at the entrance desk to help navigate the nearly 30 separate collections housed within 1,400 rooms. It is so vast that it is impossible to see all of the sections in one visit, so choose your favourite route. All of the itineraries take visitors through the Sistine Chapel.

Museum history

The idea of the papal collection dates to the early 1500s with Pope Julius II, who started by adding Classical statuary to the courtyard of the Belvedere Palace. In the same years he commissioned Raphael to redecorate his private apartments, Bramante to start construction of the new St Peter's, and Michelangelo to fresco the ceiling of the Sistine Chapel, setting a precedent for future popes. The Vatican Museums were opened to the public in the 18th century.

Pinacoteca

On entering there is a choice of directions to follow. To the right, facing west past the terrace, is the chronologically arranged **Pinacoteca** (Picture Gallery). Of note is the *Stefaneschi Triptych* dating from 1298 by Giotto (better known for his frescoes in Florence). The altarpiece was commissioned for the main altar of the old Constantinian Basilica of St Peter's. Further along are some lovely fresco fragments by Melozzo da **Forlì**, followed by three stunning altarpieces by Raphael. The two early works, *The Coronation of the Virgin* of 1503 and the *Madonna of Foligno* of 1511, are contrasted with the massive central panel of *The Transfiguration* of 1520. This was his last project and it clearly shows the influence of Michelangelo.

Successive rooms display an unfinished work by Leonardo da Vinci, some Titians and large paintings on canvas from the 1600s. Particularly interesting are Guido Reni's *Crucifixion of St Peter* and Caravaggio's unconventional *Entombment*.

Cortile della Pigna and Chiaramonti Museum

Leaving the Pinacoteca, retrace your steps east to the central **Cortile della Pigna** (Pinecone Court). This open courtyard is named after the colossal bronze pinecone, displayed in a niche. The grand scale of the new St Peter's dwarfed even this massive drinking fountain, and it was moved to its present location in 1608.

Giuseppe Momo's spiral ramp

At the far edge is the corridor of the **Museo Chiaramonti**. The static display, with original numbering system, was first laid out by Antonio Canova and shows statues of emperors and gods, and portrait busts. Further down the gallery is the entrance to the **Braccio Nuovo** section, displaying the famous *Augustus of Prima Porta*. The staircase leads into both the Egyptian Museum and Belvedere Court.

Belvedere Court

Bramante's magnificent Cortile del Belvedere (Belvedere Court) and the Museo Pio-Clementino house some of the world's most famous Classical sculptures. This is the nucleus of Julius II's collections.

Both the exquisitely proportioned *Apollo Belvedere*, and the dynamic *Laocoön* figure group, are showcased in side niches of the Octagonal Court. Further along is the Hellenistic *Belvedere Torso*, which hugely influenced Michelangelo's work. At the centre of the Sala Rotunda (round room) is a porphyry basin from the Emperor Nero's house.

The corridors

Following the stairs and the flow of traffic takes you through a series of decorated corridors. The **Gallery of the Candelabra** is full of ancient Roman sculpture, which connects to the darkened **Gallery of the Tapestries**. The tapestries at the left side were made under the Flemish master weaver, Pieter Van Aelst, from incredible full-scale cartoons sent from Raphael's studio.

Through the doors is the lengthy **Corridor of Maps** commissioned by Pope Gregory XIII in 1580, and based on the work of cartographer Ignazio Danti. The route continues through several decorative rooms that lead into the apartments of Julius II.

Raphael Rooms

This series of rooms was remodelled by Raphael for the private use of Pope Julius II. They include the *Room of Constantine* and the *Expulsion of Heliodorius from the Temple*. The masterpiece is the reading room, called the **Stanza della Segnatura** (Room of the Signature). Raphael's frescoes carry out a philosophical dialogue across the space. The *Disputation of the Holy Sacrament*, depicting a philosophical discussion of the spiritual truths, is juxtaposed with his masterpiece the *School of Athens*, a discussion of the tangible and intangible nature of philosophy. The central figures show Plato (left) with Leonardo da Vinci's face, and Aristotle (right) with hand extended.

Sistine Chapel

More is probably written about the decoration of the **Capella Sistina 5** than any other building in the world. The fortress-like chapel was started in 1475 under Pope Sixtus IV della Rovere, and great Renaissance painters, including Sandro Botticelli, Domenico Ghirlandaio and Pietro Perugino, executed the first

Pinacoteca in the Vatican

Sala della Biga, Vatican Museums

phase of decoration. These wall frescoes illustrate scenes from the *Life of Moses and Life of Christ*. The ceiling decoration was commissioned in 1508 by Pope Julius II della Rovere (nephew of Sixtus IV). Michelangelo was given the task of creating a monumental image covering an area of 500 sq m (5,400 sq ft). The nine scenes from Genesis represent the *Separation of Light from Dark, Creation of the Sun and Moon, Separation of the Waters, Creation of Adam, Creation of Eve, Expulsion from Eden, Sacrifice of Noah, The Great Flood* and *Deluge and Drunkenness of Noah*.

Nearly 30 years later, Michelangelo was again commissioned to create the fresco on the altar wall for Pope Clement VII de Medici. The tumultuous portrayal of the *Last Judgement* has been considered both a supreme masterpiece and an affront to the church.

Library and spiral ramp

The exit from the Sistine Chapel generally passes by the entrance to the Vatican Library (closed to the public). The long corridor will bring you to the main exit, down the beautiful spiral ramp designed by Giuseppe Momo in 1932. For a meal, try **Il Bar Sotto Il Mare**, see ❹, a few minutes' walk north from the museum entrance.

Food and drink

❶ TRE PUPAZZI
Borgo Pio 183; tel: 06-6880 3220; http:// ristorantetrepupazzi.it; Mon–Sat noon–3pm, 7–11pm; €€
This excellent and inexpensive restaurant has been serving local favourites since it opened as a tavern in the 17th century, but now also offers Portuguese dishes thanks to the owner's Portuguese wife. They specialise in baked dishes and veal.

❷ DA BENITO E GILBERTO
Via del Falco 19; tel: 06-686 7769; www. benitoegilberto.it; Tue–Sat noon–3pm, 7–11pm; €€
This elegant spot serves fresh, simply prepared seafood dishes. It is well known for its oysters which are served in a variety of ways. Classic Italian desserts are also on the menu, such as panna cotta and tiramisu.

❸ GELATERIA DEI GRACCHI
Via dei Gracchi 272; tel: 06-321 6668; www. gelateriadeigracchi.it; daily noon–late; €
Considered one of Rome's best gelaterias. A large variety of inventive flavours, homemade with natural ingredients. Try the extra-dark chocolate.

❹ IL BAR SOTTO IL MARE
Via Tunisi 27; tel: 06-3972 8413; Tue–Sun lunch and dinner, Mon dinner only; €€
A welcoming fish restaurant serving excellent seafood at affordable prices. The waiters speak little or no English, but the service is friendly and attentive nevertheless.

Exploring the Castel Sant'Angelo

CASTEL SANT'ANGELO TO THE GIANICOLO

This route showcases some of the city's best views and vantage points. Starting with the Castel Sant'Angelo, down the elegant Via Giulia, to the top of the Janiculum Hill. The route includes a stop to see some of Raphael's best-kept works.

DISTANCE: 3.25km (2.25 miles)
TIME: A full day
START: Castel Sant'Angelo
END: Piazzale Giuseppe Garibaldi
POINTS TO NOTE: There is a lot to see on this route, and it is not intended that you visit every museum. Plan this route for the morning if you are considering visiting the Villa Farnesina, as it is closed in the afternoon. This route ends with a rewarding but uphill walk that includes stairs. Children usually like this route.

CASTEL SANT'ANGELO

On the left bank near the Vatican is the imposing, circular, brick **Castel Sant'Angelo ❶** (Lungotevere Castello 50; http://castelsantangelo.benicul turali.it; Tue–Sun 9am–7.30pm). The building dates from AD 138, when it served as the grand-scale mausoleum for the Emperor Hadrian and his family. The mausoleum was converted into a fortress during the early 5th century, and was later given the name Castel

Sant'Angelo by Pope Gregory the Great in 590. It has since been used as a prison, and papal hideout during times of siege. A *passetto* (hidden corridor) was added in the 1270s allowing for safe passage between St Peter's and chambers inside the Castello.

Highlights

The museum of the Castel Sant' Angelo now displays artefacts from multiple periods of Roman history. The papal chambers are reached by the ancient ramp that survives from the original structure. Look for the Renaissance, hand-operated, wooden lift built for papal use, and Pope Clement VII's tiny frescoed bathroom by Giulio Romano.

The second and third floors house tapestry, paintings, and fresco. The terraces and café are popular destinations within the castle, and offer panoramic views of the nearby dome of St Peter's.

Ponte Sant'Angelo

Exit the Castel Sant'Angelo and cross the Tiber river at the bustling footbridge of **Ponte Sant'Angelo ❷**. This is one

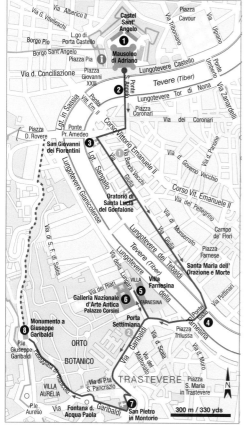

Castel Sant'Angelo

View from the castle ramparts

of the prettiest bridges in the city. The decorated walk was made to Bernini's design in the 1680s, to revamp Hadrian's original bridge.

Traverse the zebra crossing, and continue straight along the Via del Banco di Santo Spirito until it opens onto the busy Corso Vittorio Emanuele II. Cross over to the tiny Via del Consolato and continue southeast to the long and elegant Via Giulia, on the left.

VIA GIULIA

The street of **Via Giulia** is one of Rome's most prestigious addresses, dating from the early 16th century. Pope Julius II (best known for hiring Michelangelo to decorate the ceiling of the Sistine Chapel) commissioned the architect Donato Bramante to create the first straight thoroughfare through the congested medieval alleys surrounding Campo de' Fiori. It is now home to antiques shops, galleries and bars nestled between the palaces and courtyards.

San Giovanni dei Fiorentini

Directly across from Via del Consolato, at the start of the Via Giulia, is the Florentine church of **San Giovanni dei Fiorentini** ❸ (daily 7.30am–noon, 5–7pm), started

Orto Botanico

in 1509 and designed by papal architects Sangallo, Sansovino and della Porta. Inside is an impressive Baroque altar by Bernini's infamous rival Francesco Borromini.

Towards the Ponte Sisto

Heading southeast along the Via Giulia you pass some fine examples of Renaissance palazzi. There are also some nice places to stop for a drink along the way, including **Caffè Perù**, see ❶.

On the right, down the Via del Gonfalone, is the **Oratorio di Santa Lucia del Gonfalone**, which often has summer concerts. Two streets down, turn right (west) into the small Vicolo delle Prigioni (lane of the prisons), and you'll see the old prisons built in 1655 by Pope Innocent X Pamphilj.

Further along the Via Giulia on the right (directly across from the Via dei Farnesi) is the macabre church of Santa Maria dell' Orazione e Morte (St Mary of Prayer and Death).

At the end of the Via Giulia, just past the **Fontana del Mascherone** (big mask) is the footbridge of the **Ponte Sisto ❹**, over the Tiber river.

MONTE DEL GIANICOLO

The current form of the Ponte Sisto was constructed in 1471 by Pope Sixtus IV as a grand entry into the neighbourhood of **Trastevere** (see page 74).

Cross the Piazza Trilussa, and west of the piazza along the Via di Ponte Sisto turn right onto the Via della Lungara, passing through the arch of the Renaissance **Porta Settimiana**.

Villa Farnesina

Look to the right for the entrance to the small but stunning **Villa Farnesina ❺** (Via della Lungara 230; Mon–Sat 9am–2pm), built in 1511 by Baldassarre Peruzzi for the banking mogul Agostino Chigi (Pope Julius II's primary financier). The real treasure is Raphael's fresco of *Cupid and Psyche* on the ceiling of the open loggia, painted to commemorate Chigi's wedding.

Palazzo Corsini

Across from the Farnesina is the **Palazzo Corsini**, housing the **Galleria Nazionale d'Arte Antica ❻** (National Gallery of Art; Via della Lungara 10; http://galleriacorsini.beniculturali.it; Wed–Mon 8.30am–7pm). The palazzo was built

---

Botanical Gardens

The Orto Botanico (Largo Cristina di Svezia 24; Apr–Oct daily 9am–6.30pm, Nov–Mar until 5.30pm) dates from the 1880s, when it was structured out of the 17th-century gardens of the Palazzo Corsini. The stepped, terraced gardens are still in existence and have an amazing array of exotic and rare plants as well as historic species. A series of fine tiered fountains can be found along the hidden paths up the hill.

San Pietro in Montorio

for the Cardinal Riario in 1510, and completely rebuilt in 1736 under the ownership of Cardinal Corsini. It has housed numerous popes and members of nobility. The Corsini gallery includes paintings by Caravaggio, Rubens, Van Dyck and Murillo to name a few. The full collection is divided with the Palazzo Barberini (see page 56).

When you've perused the collection, retrace your steps through the Porta Settimiana, turning right up the Via Giuseppe Garibaldi. Along this street are two great restaurants: **In Vino Veritas**, see ❷, is located near the bottom of the hill and is a great spot for a relaxing drink and refuel, while **Antica Pesa** (see page 120) is a good place to return to for dinner.

San Pietro in Montorio and the Tempietto

Continue up Via Garibaldi to the church of Santa Maria dei Sette Dolori. To the right of the church is a stairway that brings you up to the piazza and the church of **San Pietro in Montorio** ❼ (www.sanpietroinmontorio.it; 8.30am–noon, 3–4pm), remodelled in the late 15th century by order from Queen Isabella and Ferdinand of Spain.

For a glimpse of the most-visited monument at the church, look in to the narrow cloister. There you will find Bramante's **Tempietto** (courtyard of San Pietro in Montorio), built in 1502 to mark the traditional spot of St Peter's martyrdom and considered the first building of the Renaissance.

Piazzale Giuseppe Garibaldi

Further up the hill is the **Fontana dell'Acqua Paola** commissioned by the Pope Paul V Borghese in 1612, in honour of the reopening of the ancient aqueduct built by Emperor Trajan in 109. Continue along the upper route of the Paseggiata di Gianicolo to see some of Rome's most breathtaking views from the **Piazzale Giuseppe Garibaldi** ❽.

To descend, continue north along the Paseggiata di Gianicolo, arriving at the Piazza della Rovere near the Vatican; alternatively, retrace your steps down to Trastevere. Note, bus 870 from Piazzale Garibaldi runs north along the ridge to Ponte Principe Amedeo.

Food and drink

❶ CAFFÈ PERÙ

Via di Monserrato 46; tel: 06-687 9548; Mon–Sat 7am–2am, Sun 8.30am–5pm; €

This neighbourhood bar with tables on the street serves great cappuccinos as well as cocktails and other drinks.

❷ IN VINO VERITAS

Via Garibaldi 2A; tel: 388 758 3772; daily 7pm–2am; €€

A great spot to enjoy some wine and Italian style charcuterie in a friendly and cosy atmosphere. Every Friday evening there is live music.

Area Sacra dell'Argentina

JEWISH QUARTER AND TRASTEVERE

This route connects two of Rome's most characterful medieval neighbourhoods: the Jewish Quarter, with its ancient Roman roots, and lively Trastevere, with its bohemian heart. Both have been home to fringe cultures for centuries.

DISTANCE: 3km (2 miles)
TIME: A half day
START: Largo di Torre Argentina
END: Piazza Trilussa
POINTS TO NOTE: Trastevere, where this route ends, is an ideal place for an evening drink or dinner. Consider this route for an afternoon and finish as the neighbourhood comes to life.

TORRE ARGENTINA

The route begins at the centre of the traffic-clogged **Largo di Torre Argentina ❶**, a piazza with a subterranean archaeological area called the **Area Sacra dell' Argentina**. The remains of the four 3rd-century BC temples were only discovered and excavated in the 1920s. This area gives some impression of the scale of ancient Roman buildings and the level of the original streets. At the southwest side are the headquarters of the cat sanctuary, whose inhabitants can be found draped about the ancient ruins.

JEWISH QUARTER

Leave the piazza from the southeast corner along little Via Paganica. This will bring you to the northern edge of the Jewish ghetto (the quarter between the Monte dei Cenci and the Teatro di Marcello, see page 39), home to one of Europe's oldest communities of Jewish families. The ghetto was walled in by the papacy in 1556, although the walls were torn down following the Unification of Italy. Via Paganica opens onto the diminutive Piazza Mattei with the **Fontana delle Tartarughe ❷** (The Turtle Fountain), completed in 1585 to designs by Giacomo della Porta.

Head east along the Via dei Funari into the lanes of the ghetto; keep right at the piazza, following the Vicolo di Campitelli, through the arch and onto the back of the Teatro di Marcello.

Portico d'Ottavia

Coming around the archaeological area dominated by the Teatro di Marcello, you will find the ruined **Portico d'Ottavia ❸**, the entrance to a colonnaded walkway built in 147 BC by Augustus to display

Religious symbols   *Fountain of the Tortoises*

statues captured from Greece. It was dedicated to his sister Ottavia, the unlucky wife of Marc Antony. By the 18th century the ruins of the Portico were home to a fish market, and it is recognisable in many genre paintings of the period. **Da Giggetto**, see ①, makes a good pit stop here.

Palazzo Cenci

Cross the piazza created along the Via del Portico d'Ottavia into the heart of the Jewish Quarter, to the **Piazza delle Cinque Scole** ④, recognisable by the basin fountain at the back of the **Palazzo Cenci**. The palace was once home

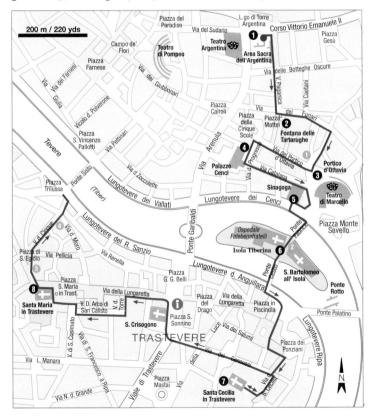

Piazza Santa Maria in Trastevere

to a powerful dynasty, whose tragedies were written about in Percy Bysshe Shelley's drama *The Cenci*.

Synagogue

Head east away from the palace, and, at the end of the Via Catalana, is the **Sinagoga** ❺ with the adjacent Museo Ebraico (Synagogue; Lungotevere dei Cenci; www.museoebraico.roma.it; Sun–Thu 10am–5pm, until 6pm in summer, Fri 9am–2pm, until 4pm in summer; tours hourly). It was constructed in 1904, after the Unification of Italy, as a symbol of newfound freedom, and has an Art Nouveau interior and an unusual aluminium square dome.

TIBER ISLAND

Cross over the Lungotevere dei Cenci and make your way over the oldest-standing bridge in Rome, the **Ponte Fabricio** (built in 62 BC). You will come

to the **Isola Tiberina** ❻ (Tiber Island), the smallest inhabited island in the world. A temple to Aesculapius, the Greek god of medicine, once stood on the island. There has been a church and hospital on this site for centuries.

In the middle of the island is the wonderful **Sora Lella**, see ❷. During the summer, the wide sloping banks are home to festivals, outdoor eateries and beer gardens. From the south side of this lower level it is possible to see the ancient **Ponte Rotto** (Broken Bridge), the carved remains of Rome's first stone bridge.

TRASTEVERE

Leaving the island, cross into Trastevere, meaning 'across the Tevere' (the Italian name for the Tiber river). Many of the street names here reflect their original function.

Santa Cecilia in Trastevere

From the Ponte Cestio, cross the Lungotevere Anguillara and turn left along the river, then turn right (southwest) past the car park along the Via Titta Scarpetta to the Via dei Salumi (Street of Salami). Turn left here and take the second right, Via Vascellari. Continue until you reach the church of **Santa Cecilia in Trastevere** ❼ (daily 10am–12.30pm and 4–6pm; choir and Cavallini frescoes: Mon–Fri 10am–12.30pm). This late-4th-century church is dedicated to St Cecilia, one of the early martyrs. The current structure dates primarily from the 12th century, with some original elements, and the interior

The cats of Rome

Rome is home to hundreds of thousands of stray cats living in its ruins. In recent years the cats have been counted, fed, vaccinated, neutered and clipped through a charity service at Largo di Torre Argentina (www.gattidiroma.net; Mon–Fri noon–6pm, Sat–Sun 11am–6pm). The animal care runs on international donations. Many cats are available for adoption.

Ponte Cestio   *Mosaics, Santa Maria in Trastevere*

has impressive mosaics from the period. Look for the fragmentary *Last Judgement* frescoes by Pietro Cavallini in the galley, and an incredible Baroque sculpture of *Santa Cecilia* by Stefano Maderno below the altar.

Heart of Trastevere

Double back along the Via di Santa Cecilia, then turn left (west) along the Via dei Genovesi. When you reach the Viale di Trastevere, turn right and head past the church of San Crisogano, then turn left into Via della Lungaretta. This road acts as the main thoroughfare into central Trastevere. For a taste of the characteristic side streets turn left onto the Vicolo della Torre and follow the Via dell'Arco di San Calisto until you arrive at the piazza.

Santa Maria in Trastevere

The focal point of the piazza is the basilica of **Santa Maria in Trastevere** ❽ (daily 7.30am–9pm). It is one of the earliest Christian churches, dating from the 3rd century, although, like many others in Rome, it was rebuilt in the 12th century. The granite columns along the nave were taken as spoils from the Baths of Caracalla (see page 37). The wonderful mosaics of the Virgin Mary on the front of the church give an indication of the beauty and quality of the decoration to be found within. Of note are the apse mosaics that complement Cavallini's series of the *Life of the Virgin* dating back to 1291.

There are many good restaurants, in this area, including the **Ombre Rosse**, see ❸, or **Enoteca Ferrara**, see ❹.

Food and drink

❶ DA GIGGETTO

Via del Portico d'Ottavia 21; tel: 06-686 1105; Tue–Sun 12.30–3pm, 7–11pm; €€
With the feel of a retro film set, this place has a diverse enough menu for any tastes, yet still focuses on Roman traditional dishes, of which the signature is crispy artichokes.

❷ SORA LELLA

Via di Ponte Quattro Capi 16; tel: 06-686 1610; daily 12.45–2.50pm, 7.30–11pm; €€€
This upmarket trattoria serves traditional Roman fare with a twist and is always packed.

❸ OMBRE ROSSE

Piazza di Sant'Egidio 12; tel: 06-588 4155; https://ombrerosseintrastevere.it; daily 10am–2am; €
Attractive dark wood, nice outdoor seating, a small menu and a great drinks selection makes this perfect for a break.

❹ ENOTECA FERRARA

Piazza Trilussa 41; tel: 06-5833 3920; www.enotecaferrara.it; daily 7.30pm–midnight, Sun 1–3.30pm also; €€
This elegant enoteca is the place to go for some fabulous wine accompanied by the staples of Roman cuisine, such as tonnarelli cacio e pepe, or gnocchi with spinach and ricotta.

Orange trees in Parco Savello

AVENTINO AND TESTACCIO

Just south of the Palatine are the quarters of Aventino and Testaccio. Centrally located, rich in history, and surprisingly off the beaten track, the aristocratic Aventine Hill, with its great setting and cool breezes, looks over the working-class district of Testaccio, known for its markets and nightlife.

DISTANCE: 4km (2.5 miles)
TIME: A half day
START: Circo Massimo metro
END: Centrale Montemartini
POINTS TO NOTE: This itinerary, though not difficult, covers a lot of ground. Consider stopping for lunch along the way or picking up a picnic at the food market in Testaccio. The route ends at the wonderful Centrale Montemartini museum; though located along an industrial boulevard, it is well connected for the return journey to the centre. You can catch a bus just to the north along Via Ostiense, or the metro (Piramide) is only a short walk further.

This route starts with a breath of fresh air on the Aventine Hill before continuing into the working-class Testaccio, one of the city's most dynamic areas. The latter doesn't feature on many tourist itineraries, but it's worth a visit before it goes the way of Trastevere and becomes trendy, changing its character for good.

AVENTINO

Starting at the metro station named after the **Circo Massimo** (see page 37), head northwest along the Via del Circo Massimo to the circular Piazzale Ugo La Malfa. The Via di Valle Murcia leads up the Aventino through a rose garden. The Aventino is one of the seven hills of Rome, and has been inhabited by patrician families since the age of the Republic. Some of the regal feeling is retained in its leafy streets and walled gardens, and the chaos of the nearby traffic has not yet overwhelmed this hilltop oasis.

Parco Savello and Santa Sabina

At the summit of the slope is the church of Santa Sabina. In front is the Piazza Pietro d'Illiria (used as a car park), on the right of which is an arched entry into the beautiful **orangery ❶** (Giardino degli Aranci), also known as the **Parco Savello**. The garden was once part of the Savello family fortress of the 12th century. Now it is full of families with small children and couples having photos taken under the orange trees that are characteristic of Rome.

Outside the Priory of Malta   *View to St Peter's, Priory of Malta*

The adjacent church of **Santa Sabina ②** (Piazza Pietro d'Illiria 1; daily 7.15am–8pm) is one of the most popular wedding locations in the city. The 5th-century interior is quite simple, with a light airy feeling created by the open space, and beautifully set Corinthian columns and clear glass windows. The rare cypress wood doors from the 420s (at the left entry) show scenes from the New Testament, depicting one of the first known representations of the crucifixion. In the portico are several inscribed floor tombs, made from ancient marble sarcophagi. This early method of recycling, which can be seen in medieval churches throughout Rome, preserved the original carvings; a clever rotating stand allows for viewing both sides.

Priory of Malta and Sant'Anselmo

At the far end of the summit is the Piazza dei Cavalieri di Malta (Knights of Malta) with its cypress-lined wall. On the piazza is the **Priorato di Malta ③**. This secretive chivalric order was founded in 1050, and continues to operate as a charitable organisation. The priory is closed to the public, but the main draw is their keyhole. Take a peek through it and you'll see the faraway dome of St Peter's appear as if it were in the garden. The piazza and the doorway were designed by the fantastical 18th-century printmaker, Gian Battista Piranesi.

The monastic building at the far side of the piazza is the church of **Sant'Anselmo ④** (Piazza Cavalieri di Malta 5; www.santanselmo.net; open daily), constructed in 1900 as the seat of the Rule of St Benedict. The architecture is a strange mixture of neo-Gothic and Romanesque.

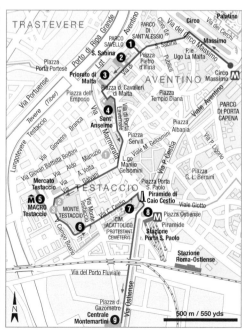

Gastronomia Volpetti

Perhaps the most interesting thing is the **Benedictine shop**, which sells teas, medicinal herbs, liqueurs and honeys produced by the Benedictines. The monks sing a Gregorian-style vespers at sunset on most evenings as well as on Sunday mornings.

TESTACCIO

Take the Via di Porta Lavernale to drop down into Testaccio. Continue to the foot of the hill and cross the clogged artery of the Via Marmorata to Via Galvani. A few streets up Via Marmorata is the family-run **Gastronomia Volpetti**, one of the best Italian delicatessens in the city, see ❶.

Monte Testaccio

Continue along the Via Galvani past several trendy nightclubs and bars. There is a noticeable contrast between the solemn hillside of the Aventino, and the flat regular lanes of the Testaccio. Most of the current residential Testaccio was built in the 19th century, but, like all of Rome, it has an older history. The neighbourhood is named after the **Monte Testaccio** (Hill of Shards), which is a 35m (115ft) -high hill created from bits of broken pottery. The low-lying flats of the area were used from 140 BC to about AD 250 to unload the millions of amphorae and supplies coming up river to the capital. When the great jars of olive oil were decanted they were flung onto the pile. The function of the neighbourhood as a major gateway for food and goods lasted until the mid-1970s when the city's congestion forced suppliers to the outlying suburbs.

Mattatoio and MACRO Testaccio

At the end of the street is the entrance to what was once the **Mattatoio** (slaughterhouse) of Rome. The massive complex closed in 1975 and was abandoned for over a decade. The eerie architecture and uncharacteristic warehouse spaces are now home to Roma Tre (University of Rome), the Villaggio Globale (a summer venue for arts, music and fringe gay scene), the Città dell'Altra Economia (a space for local food with an occasional organic market and a restaurant) and the contemporary art museum **MACRO Testaccio** ❺ (Piazza Orazio Giustiniani 4; www.museomacro.org; Tue–Sun 2–8pm, open for exhibitions only). The space exhibits edgy, and often unknown, contemporary artists and is one of the few venues for performance and installation art.

Just around the corner from the entrance of MACRO Testaccio is **Ristorante Pecorino**, a classic Roman restaurant serving delicious food, see ❷. In Via Galvani, before the main entrance of MACRO Testaccio, is the Mercato Testaccio, the main daily produce market of the area, and also one of the best. Next door is **Trattoria Checchino dal 1887**, see ❸, one of the better restaurants of the area.

Where the road forks, head left past the car park along the **Via Monte Testaccio** ❻. There are clubs and bars along this street that have been carved

MACRO Testaccio   Centrale Montemartini

out of the millions of shards of pottery that make up the hillside.

Protestant cemetery and the pyramid

At the far side walk up the steps and cross the Via Nicola Zabaglia to the Via Caio Cestio, where you will find the **Cimitero Acattolico 7** (Protestant Cemetery; www.cemeterytrome.it; Mon–Sat 9am–4.30pm, Sun 9am–12.30pm). This dilapidated burial ground has been a favourite of anglophiles since the 19th century. The most famous graves here are those of the Romantic poets John Keats and Percy Bysshe Shelley, who died within a year of each other.

At one edge of the cemetery is Rome's pyramid, known as the **Piramide di Caio Cestio 8**. This monument was constructed as a mausoleum for Caius Cestius in 18 BC, at a time when Egyptian decoration was the fashion.

Centrale Montemartini

Just to the south is Via Ostiense. Take a 10-minute walk down this road and you come to the **Centrale Montemartini**, one of Rome's most intriguing museums. The road itself is built up and unappealing, but the rewards at the end are worth making the effort. (Note that buses 23 or 769 running south along the Via Ostiense stop at the museum.)

The Museo della Centrale Montemartini 9 (Via Ostiense 106; www.centralemontemartini.org; Tue–Sun 9am–7pm) is a winning marriage of art and technology, old and new. Ancient sculpture is exhibited in a converted 1894 power station. The museum opened in 1997 as a temporary exhibition space for 400 sculptures from the Capitoline Museums. The exhibition was so successful that it has become a permanent extension of the museums.

Food and drink

1 GASTRONOMIA VOLPETTI
Via Marmorata 47; tel: 06-574 2352; www.volpetti.com; Mon–Fri 8.30am–2pm, 4.30–8.15pm, Sat 8.30am–8.30pm; €€
This delicatessen has some of the finest meats, cheeses and pastas in the city. It is takeaway only, but you can try their food at Volpetti Più round the corner at Via Alessandro Volta 8.

2 RISTORANTE PECORINO
Via Galvani, 64; tel: 06-5725 0539; Tue–Sun 12.30–2.30pm, 8–11pm; €€
A vibrant crowd fills this neighbourhood restaurant that serves classic dishes in a cosy setting.

3 TRATTORIA CHECCHINO DAL 1887
Via di Monte Testaccio 30; tel: 06-574 3816; www.checchino-dal-1887.com; Tue–Sat 12.30–3pm, 8–11.45pm; €€€
Reserve here, as a stream of regulars come for the excellent meat dishes. The wine list is top, but the fun part is going down into the cantina to have a look around, including at the ancient amphorae.

Outside San Clemente

SAN GIOVANNI AND ESQUILINO

The adjacent areas of San Giovanni and the Esquiline Hill are home to some of Rome's finest churches, including the modest San Clemente, tiny Santa Prassede, imposing San Giovanni in Laterano and grand Santa Maria Maggiore.

> **DISTANCE:** 2.5km (1.5 miles)
> **TIME:** A half day
> **START:** San Clemente
> **END:** Santa Maria Maggiore
> **POINTS TO NOTE:** If this route is started in the morning, it can easily be followed by route 13 for a full day. If you choose to start in the afternoon, consider having lunch first in the San Clemente area.

The route starts behind the Colosseum at San Clemente, and continues to San Giovanni in Laterano, the world's ecumenical mother church. There are good choices for lunch spots in San Clemente such as **Pizzeria Naumachia**, see ❶, or **Colosseo 'Luzzi'**, see ❷.

SAN CLEMENTE

The unpretentious basilica of **San Clemente** ❶ (main entrance Piazza San Clemente; www.basilicasanclemente.com; Mon–Fri 9am–12.30pm, 3–6pm, Sat–Sun noon–6pm; charge for excavations) is an open door into one of Rome's best time capsules. Its walls contain three separate houses of worship, built one upon the other and spanning a period of nearly two thousand years. The street-level building dates to the 12th century, incorporating some 6th-century sections, and has been run by an order of Irish Dominicans since the 17th century.

Not to be missed are the marble choir enclosure and the large apse mosaics from the 1180s, depicting the *Triumph of the Cross* as a twisting tree of life. The restored Renaissance chapel to St Catherine of Alexandria contains fine 15th-century frescoes by Masolino (best known for his collaboration on the Brancacci Chapel in Florence).

Lower levels

Through the gift shop are the stairs down to the excavations (tickets can be purchased here). At the lower level is the original 4th-century church, with well-preserved fragments of the 11th-century frescoes depicting the miracles of St Clement. Further down is an intact late 2nd-century temple to the pagan god

Santi Quattro Coronati   San Giovanni in Laterano

Mithras (Mithraism, associated with bull sacrifice and masculine potency, was a popular religious cult introduced to Rome through the legions in Asia Minor) and the adjacent apartments used for clandestine Christian worship. The constant sound of rushing water is the Cloaca Maxima, or ancient sewer, which is still in use.

Monastery of Santi Quattro Coronati

From San Clemente, head along the Via dei Querceti, then turn left up the hill onto the Via dei SS. Quattro, where, at No. 20, you will find the entrance to the secluded monastery of **Santi Quattro Coronati** ❷ (Mon–Sat 9.30–11.30am, 3.30–5.30pm; charge for oratory), one of the city's oldest churches. This hidden treasure is still run by cloistered Augustinian nuns. Of note are the Romanesque cloister and the frescoes in the Oratory of Pope St Sylvester, depicting the life of Emperor Constantine. Entrance is granted by ringing the bell, and a nun will pass you a key through the double blind.

SAN GIOVANNI

Continue east to the piazza at the side of the Lateran Palaces. These were the first official papal residences, used from the 4th century until the development of the Vatican.

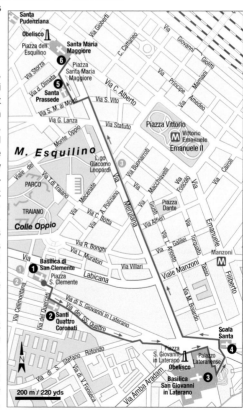

Mercato Esquilino

San Giovanni in Laterano

Continue around Rome's largest standing obelisk, brought from the Temple of Amun at Karnak. On the opposite side of the cluster of buildings, facing east, is the front of the basilica of **San Giovanni in Laterano** ❸ (www.vatican.va; 7am–6.30pm. cloister: daily 9am–6pm).

San Giovanni is officially the first Christian basilica, and the cathedral of the diocese of Rome, of which the Pope is bishop. As it houses the papal throne, the church holds a higher spiritual significance than St Peter's itself. San Giovanni is dedicated to Our Saviour and also to St John the Baptist and St John the Evangelist.

The church, which has been rebuilt multiple times, has a rich history and many highlights. At the main entrance, in the bold 18th-century facade, are the original bronze doors, taken from the Curia in the Forum. The massive Baroque statues of the 12 Apostles line the support columns of the nave and contrast with the 14th-century *baldacchino* covering the papal altar. The gilt-and-coffered-wood ceiling dates from 1567. Away from the grand scale of the main church is the calming, which dates to 1230 and is decorated in the Cosmatesque style.

Scala Santa

Across the piazza is the entrance to the **Scala Santa** ❹ (Apr–Sept daily 6am–2pm and 3–6.30pm, until 7pm in summer), believed to be the 28 steps Christ ascended in Pontius Pilate's house. Emperor Constantine's mother, St Helena, brought the stairs to Rome as one of the first holy relics. Bus-loads of devout pilgrims still climb up on their knees.

ESQUILINO

Just north of the obelisk is the long, tree-lined Via Merulana, which runs up the western slope of the Esquiline Hill. This residential area is full of shops selling cheeses, cured meats and designer furniture. The bakery **Panella**, see ❸, is perfect for a treat along the way.

Santa Prassede

Towards the top of Via Merulana, turn left at Via San Martino ai Monti, then right onto the Via Santa Prassede, and you will reach the unassuming **Santa Pras-**

Ethnic Esquilino

The Renaissance villas that once covered the Esquiline were demolished in the 1870s to make way for Rome's new neighbourhood, with the focal point being the Piazza Vittorio Emanuele II, named after the new king. However, the plan failed to attract the growing middle classes, and the area fell into decline. The area is now home to a thriving international community, with the Chinese and Asian population notably carving out a niche here. At Via Lamarmora's outdoor vegetable-and-fish market, for example, Italian fresh produce has been replaced with halal meats, spices and exotic African fruits.

Santa Prassede   *Santa Maria Maggiore*

sede **❺** (daily 7am–noon, 3–6.30pm) at
No. 9. This lovely church dates from 780,
and is dedicated to one of the daughters
of St Pudens, who was St Paul's first con-
vert to Christianity. The intricate Byzan-
tine-style mosaics depicting the sainted
family are some of the earliest, most
important in Rome. Nearby is the church
of Santa Pudenziana, Santa Prassede's
sister (see page 86).

Santa Maria Maggiore

Just round the corner is the basilica of
Santa Maria Maggiore ❻ (www.vatican.
va; daily 7am–6.45pm), one of four patri-
archal basilicas, and the only one dedicated to the Virgin Mary.

The various decorative styles of Santa
Maria Maggiore give the church a feeling
of regal elegance. Most notable are the
rich Cosmatesque floors reminiscent of
prayer rugs from Byzantium. To the left,
near the altar, is the elaborate chapel to
Pope Paul V Borghese, with a Baroque
altar containing one of the oldest icons of
the Virgin Mary.

The mosaics in the main church are
exceptional, with a series form the 430s
located along the nave depicting sto-
ries form the Old Testament. These are
located near the upper windows.

The nave decoration is complemented
by the powerful *Coronation of the Virgin*
apse mosaics from 1295, by Jacopo Torriti.
The expansive wood coffered ceiling was
added by Pope Alexander VI Borgia in the
1490s and is decorated with gold from the
New World donated by Isabella of Spain.

In the confession, below the high altar,
are the relics of the Holy Manger from
Bethlehem. Many of the Christmas traditions celebrated today originated at Santa
Maria Maggiore.

The rear side of this church is decorated
with a magnificent staircase and one of
Rome's many Egyptian obelisks. The obelisk at the centre of the Piazza Esquilino is
from the Mausoleum of Augustus.

Food and drink

❶ PIZZERIA NAUMACHIA
Via Celimontana 7; tel: 06-700 2764;
www.naumachiaroma.com; daily 11am–
midnight; €€
A good pasta and wood-oven pizza place
near the Colosseum with a large seating area
on the lower floor.

❷ RISTORANTE COLOSSEO "LUZZI"
Via di S. Giovanni in Laterano 88; tel: 06-709
6332; Thu–Tue noon–midnight; €€
Simple, delicious pizzas and pastas are
served in a relaxed environment at this
restaurant that has been open since 1945.

❸ PANELLA
Via Merulana 54; tel: 06-487 2435; www.
panellaroma.com; Mon–Sat 7am–11pm,
Sun 7am–9pm; €
This neighbourhood bakery, complete with
beautiful garden, has been selling breads,
cakes, biscuits, crêpes, savoury filo bundles
and mini pizzas, as well as coffee since 1929.

Diocletian Complex

DIOCLETIAN COMPLEX AND MONTI

This route starts with the national archaeological collections at the Baths of Diocletian, then continues down into the ancient streets of the Rione Monti neighbourhood and leads up to the pilgrim church of San Pietro in Vincoli.

DISTANCE: 3km (2 miles)
TIME: A half day
START: Diocletian Complex
END: San Pietro in Vincoli
POINTS TO NOTE: This is an easy route incorporating several archaeological collections. The starting point is located only a few streets away from route 12, and the two can be paired for a full-day itinerary. Two of the museums comprising the Museo Nazionale Romano are covered in this route. Tickets are valid for all four museums over a three-day period.

DIOCLETIAN COMPLEX

Rome's richest collection of archaeological artefacts has been housed in the remains of the **Terme di Diocleziano** since the 1870s. The **Museo Nazionale Romano** ❶ (Roman National Museums; Viale Enrico de Nicola 78; www.museona zionaleromano.beniculturali.it; Tue–Sun 9am–7.30pm) shares its collections with three other spaces, the nearby Pala-

zzo Massimo, Palazzo Altemps, and the Crypta Balbi. The most historic group of artefacts is exhibited in the ruins of the magnificent terme, or bath complex.

History of the baths

Built by the Emperor Diocletian in 306, the baths served up to 3,000 visitors at one time. In addition to the requisite bathing areas, heated to different temperatures with elaborate subterranean chambers, there were rooms for steam and a large *natatio* (open-air pool). The ambitious *terme* had separate spaces for meetings, dining, shopping, lecturing, temples, art exhibitions and a library. These ruins were first remodelled by Michelangelo in the 1560s, under Pope Pius IV, and his construction of a Carthusian monastery kept much of the original structure as it was.

The collection

The complex houses over 400 Classical sculptures and architectural fragments. When entering from the Via Enrico Fermi (across the street from the Termini Station), you will see the gardens and cloister with signs indicating open

Museo Nazionale Romano   *Piazza della Repubblica*

sections. Rooms I–IX contain temple statuary and decorations from the baths themselves. Rooms X–XII house major works such as the *Anadyomene Aphrodite* and the *Lance-Bearer*, and an extensive epigraph collection.

Santa Maria degli Angeli e dei Martiri

Exiting along the Viale Luigi Einaudi brings you to the brick entrance of the church of **Santa Maria degli Angeli e dei Martiri ❷** (Piazza della Repubblica; www.santamariadegliangeliroma.it; daily 7am–7.30pm). The facade is a section of Diocletian's massive complex, decorated with modern bronze doors. The church was part of the 1563 construction plan by Michelangelo, who created a vaulted transept out of the existing *frigidarium* (cool-water bath). His architectural scheme left the original structure exposed, and he even incorporated the massive granite columns into the church. Remodelling in 1749 greatly modified Michelangelo's idea, but the scale of the building remains. On the floor, running diagonally, is the meridian line added in 1702 by Francesco Bianchini under Pope Clement XI. This was designed to

check the accuracy of the new Gregorian reformation of the calendar.

Octagonal Hall

Past Santa Maria degli Angeli is the entrance to the **Aula Ottagona ❸** (Octagonal Hall; Via Giuseppe Romita 8; open for special events only), one of the few standing sections of the bath complex. The room has an octagonal oculus and was transformed into a planetarium in 1928. It now houses some of the most elegant Classical sculptures from the nearby museum.

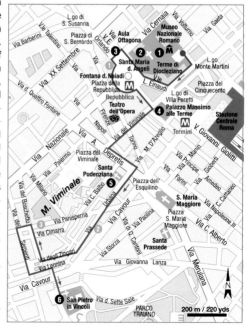

Classical sculpture at Palazzo Massimo

Cross the Piazza della Repubblica, circling around the beautiful **Fontana delle Naiadi** (Fountain of the Naiads) designed by Mario Rutelli. The Via delle Terme di Diocleziano at the far side leads to the entrance of the Palazzo Massimo.

If you fancy a snack break at this point, try backtracking along the Via Emanuele Orlando to the legendary **Dagnino**, see ❶. Continue along to the Palazzo Massimo.

PALAZZO MASSIMO

The majority of the collections of the Museo Nazionale Romano are on view at the **Palazzo Massimo alle Terme** ❹ (Largo di Villa Peretti 2; www.museona zionaleromano.beniculturali.it; Tue–Sun 9am–7.45pm; tickets from the Terme di Diocleziano are valid), opened in 1889 and now one of the world's leading Classical art museums. The antiquities collections date from the 2nd century BC through the 4th century AD.

On the lower floor is the coins section, and the ground floor is dedicated to statuary, including a bust of *Hadrian*, and the *Via Labicana Augustus*. Statuary continues on the first floor with statues of gods from Nero's summer villa. Most impressive are the rooms on the second floor with frescoes from the villa of Augustus's wife Livia.

MONTI

To continue, walk southwest along the Via del Viminale, past the **Teatro dell'Opera**, Rome's main opera house, to the Piazza del Viminale (home to the Ministry of Internal Affairs).

At the end of the street turn left. The descent along Via **Agostino** Depretis leads into the neighbourhood of **Monti** (meaning *hills*). This ancient residential area was once called the *Suburra* and was renamed in the Middle Ages for its location between the Viminale, Esquiline and Quirinale hills. Once seedy, it is now considered one of the most authentically Roman areas, with tiny alleyways and cobbled lanes dotted with boutiques and attractive restaurants. Some of the charm was wiped away under Benito Mussolini, who had about 30 percent of Monti flattened to create the **Via dei Fori Imperiali**, but the feel of the neighbourhood remains.

Santa Pudenziana

At the Piazza dell'Esquilino, where you can see the rear of Santa Maria Maggiore (see page 83), take the first right. Along Via Urbana is the tiny church of **Santa Pudenziana** ❺ (Via Urbana 160; www.stpudenziana.org; Tue–Sat 9am–noon, 3–6pm), located down the stairs at the old street level. The church is dedicated to the daughter of Pudens, a 1st-century senator. According to legend, Pudens hosted St Peter, and he and his two daughters, Pudenziana and Prassede, became early Christian converts. The church of Santa Prassede (see page 82) is nearby on the Esquiline. Both churches have early Christian decoration. The apse mosaics

Santa Pudenziana   Steps link San Pietro in Vincoli to Via Cavour

at Santa Pudenziana have been through several bouts of questionable restoration, but the scene with the Apostles in Roman togas is still mesmerising.

Shopping and food options

Continue down the hill along Via Urbana with its tiny workshops, mosaic studios, and shirt makers. Consider stopping for a break at stylish **Urbana 47**, see ②. If something more substantial is in order, turn right (west) onto the Via degli Zingari (street of the gypsies), then take a right up Via del Boschetto. This straight road is jammed with antiques stores, boutiques and trendy designers. For light fare try **Ai Tre Scalini**, see ③. **La Carbonara** (see page 121) (Mon–Sat 12.30–2.30pm and 7–11pm) is the best choice for a larger meal.

To continue the route from Via del Boschetto, turn left into Via Panisperna and left again into Via dei Serpenti, which is considered the 'main street' of Monti. Head past the main piazza with a fountain and turn left (east) into Via Leonina. This will take you past shops to a set of steps along the right. Climb the steps, cross the busy Via Cavour, and continue up the steps and through the archway on the far side to the piazza of San Pietro in Vincoli.

SAN PIETRO IN VINCOLI

The austere style of the church of **San Pietro in Vincoli** ❻ (St Peter in Chains; Piazza San Pietro in Vincoli 4; daily 8am–12.30pm, 3.30–7pm, until 6pm in winter) gives no indication of the popularity of this spot. Visitors come either to look at the reliquary housing the chains used to bind St Peter in the Mamertine Prison, or to see Michelangelo's unfinished monument to Pope Julius II. The figure of Moses, one of the proposed 47 figures from the original monument plan, is in a side chapel.

Food and drink

① DAGNINO

Galleria Esedra, Via Emanuele Orlando 75; tel: 06-481 8660; 7am–11pm; €

This 1950s-era café and pastry shop has a huge selection of Sicilian specialities such as *cannoli* and *cassata* cakes. Also does good *arancini* (fried rice balls with cheese and various fillings).

② URBANA 47

Via Urbana 47; tel: 06-4788 4006; www.urbana47.it; Wed–Mon 8am–midnight; €€

A fun café/wine bar/restaurant with a contemporary feel and a locally sourced, heavily organic menu. The wine selection (lots available by the glass) is primarily from Lazio.

③ AI TRE SCALINI

Via Panisperna 251; tel: 06-4890 7495; www.aitrescalini.org; 12pm–1am; €

This relaxed enoteca has been serving wines and simple dishes since 1895.

Arch of Drusus, Appian Way

THE APPIAN WAY

Just outside the city centre is the verdant Via Appia Antica, the 'Queen of Roads' that ran for 560km (350 miles) from Rome to the port of Brindisi on the Adriatic. This stretch of the original highway is lined with ancient tombs, ruins, sections of aqueduct and catacombs.

DISTANCE: 7km (4 miles)
TIME: A full day
START: Porta San Sebastiano
END: Villa dei Quintili
POINTS TO NOTE: This child-friendly route begins south of the city centre and requires some form of transport either at the start or later along. It is perfect for a picnic lunch and an afternoon's cycling to the sights.

Getting around

There are a number of ways to get to the ancient gateway of the Porta San Sebastiano, where this route begins. Several city buses stop along the Via Appia Antica: the 118 from Via Aventino and the 218 from Piazza San Giovanni are the most direct lines. A great way to visit the Appian Way in all its 5km (3 miles) of monuments, statues, aqueducts and nature is to rent bicycles from the Appia Antica service centre (Via Appia Antica 58/60; 06-513 5316; www.infopointappia.it). The bicycles cost €3 per hour (however the minimum rental time is 4 hours) or €15 for the whole day. Bookings online via the website.

History

The Via Appia originally ran from the Circus Maximus to Capua, and was built by the censor Appius Claudius Caecus in 312 BC. When the road was extended in 190 BC, to Brindisi, it became the gateway to the east. Eventually with the construction of the Baths of Caracalla (see page 37) and the Aurelian walls, the starting point was shifted to the Porta Appia (Porta San Sebastiano). The first section of the road was lined with villas and the mausoleums of illustrious Romans. What we now see are only small sections that connect the ruins of a few of the ancient monuments.

PORTA SAN SEBASTIANO

Start the tour at the ancient **Porta San Sebastiano ❶**, one of the few remaining gateways in the Aurelian wall. To the left of the gate is the entry to the Museo delle Mura (Museum of the Walls; www.museodellemuraroma.it; Tue–Sun

A bumpy ride   Circo di Massenzio

9am–2pm), a small museum with information about the construction of the Aurelian wall. Remains of the aqueducts and the surrounding fields are visible from the ramparts.

Visitors' centre

Past the Porta San Sebastiano to the south is the first section of the Via Appia Antica. Here it is dusty and polluted from the endless stream of cars. Continue down the road for about 800m/yds to the Visitors' Centre and Park Headquarters of the **Parco Regionale dell' Appia Antica ②** (Via Appia Antica 60; www.parcoappiaantica.it; Mon–Fri 9.30am–1pm and 2–6pm Sat–Sun 9.30am–7pm, earlier during winter months). Their free map and brochure lists about 50 different sites. Consider hiring a bicycle for the day to have access to all of the catacombs and views of the oldest parts of the road.

Further along, past the church of **Domine Quo Vadis** (which marks where, in the 1st century,

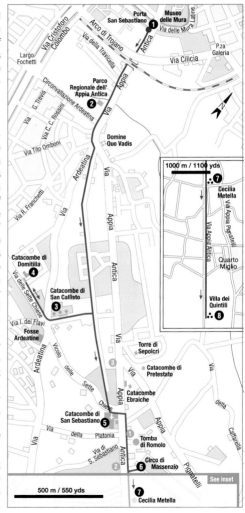

Wandering the Appian Way

the Apostle Peter was said to have met Christ), is a major fork. Keep to the central lane to continue the walk towards San Callisto.

VIA ARDEATINA

While much of the Via Appia Antica is lined with tombs and monuments, it is usually what lies below ground that is most fascinating to visitors. Kilometres of catacomb tunnels have been carved out of the volcanic tufa. Over the centuries many of the saints and early popes were buried here, and they became shrines and places of pilgrimage. The catacombs are maintained by the Pontifical Commission of Sacred Archaeology and are open to the public as part of a guided visit.

Catacombs of San Callisto
Walking south along the traffic free lane you will come to the **Catacombe di San Callisto** ❸ (Via Appia Antica 110/126; www.catacombe.roma.it; daily 9am–noon, 2–5pm). From San Callisto, walk a few minutes west through the park. Pope Saint Callixtus was the first Bishop of Rome, and, as the first Christian burial area, this catacomb housed the remains of early popes. Many of the macabre burial chambers are decorated with frescoes.

Catacombs of Domitilla
The entrance to the nearby **Catacombe di Domitilla** ❹ (No. 282; www.domitilla.info; Wed–Mon 9am–noon, 2–5pm)

is located to the west, across the Via Ardeatina on the Via delle Sette Chiese. This is the largest network of catacombs in Rome. Most of what is accessible was built between the 1st and 2nd centuries, and by the 4th century it was used as a major burial site for Christians.

World War II reminder
Along the Via Ardeatina is a sad memorial to Nazi atrocity. The Fosse Ardeatine (Via Ardeatina 174; www.mausoleofosseardeatine.it; Mon–Fri 8.15am–3.15pm, Sat–Sun until 4.45pm) marks the spot where, on 24 March 1944, 335 randomly selected Roman civilians and prisoners were murdered by firing squad as a revenge act for 32 German soldiers who had been killed in a bomb attack.

VIA APPIA ANTICA

From San Callisto, continue south through the park area to join the Via Appia Antica at the **Catacombe di San Sebastiano** ❺ (Catacombs of St Sebastian; No. 136; www.catacombe.org; Mon–Sat 10am–5pm), an extensive catacomb complex on four levels. Above is the 17th-century church to the martyred St Sebastian.

Lunch options
Nearby the church are several good restaurants, see ❶, ❷ and ❸. If you packed a picnic, consider cycling to the Appia Pignatelli and sitting under the remains of the aqueducts. From Pign-

atelli, carry on the tour in reverse, back-tracking north from the Villa dei Quintili to the Tomb of Cecilia Metella.

Circus of Maxentius
Refuelled from lunch, continue south to the **Circo di Massenzio** ❻ (Via Appia Antica 153; www.villadimassenzio.it; Tue–Sun 10am–4pm). This is the site of the magnificent stadium built by the Emperor Maxentius in 309. Both his villa and circus were constructed on the busy Via Appia to entertain sporting, military and business-men on their way out of town.

Mausoleum of Cecilia Metella
Further along the Via Appia Antica is the mausoleum of **Cecilia Metella** ❼ (Via Appia Antica 161; www.archeoroma.beniculturali.it; Tue–Sun 9am–4.30pm). This circular family tomb was built *c.*50 BC and is one of the few grand monu-ments constructed for a woman. The building survives to this day because of Pope Boniface VIII Caetani, who gave the tomb to his relatives in the early 14th century. They remodelled and used it as a fortress to exact tolls on the Via Appia Antica. Cecilia Metella is mentioned in Byron's epic poem *Childe Harold*.

Villa dei Quintili
The Via Appia Antica becomes much more rustic after this point, and it is here that you will find the tomb of Seneca and the eroded tomb of the famous Horatii. Further along are the remains of one of the largest country villas from the 2nd century. The **Villa dei Quintili** ❽ (Via Appia Nuova 1092; www.pierreci.it; Tue–Sun 9am–4pm) once belonged to the Quintili brothers who amassed great wealth as consuls. There is a shop, toi-lets and city bus 664 stop (which can take you to the Metro A station at Arco Di Travertino) here.

Food and drink

❶ CECILIA METELLA
Via Appia Antica 125; tel: 06-512 6769; www.ceciliametella.it; daily noon–3pm and 7.30–10.30pm; €€€
This busy restaurant has a pleasant atmosphere, beautiful garden seating, terrace views and serves typical Italian dishes at good prices. Reserve in summer.

❷ L'ARCHEOLOGIA
Via Appia Antica 139; tel: 06-788 0494; www.larcheologia.it; daily noon–3pm and 7.30pm–11pm; €€€
Popular with Italian tourists, this hostaria has a lovely garden and is known for its fish dishes with roasted potatoes and its wide selection of excellent wines.

❸ HOSTARIA ANTICA ROMA
Via Appia Antica 176; tel: 06-513 2888; Tue–Sun 12.15–2.45pm and 7.30–10.45pm; €€€€
This large restaurant with outdoor seating has an old-style Roman ambience, with a menu to match (lots of grilled meat).

Villa Adriana

TIVOLI'S VILLAS

Pressed against a hillside with commanding views of the plains below, Tivoli was once home to Roman emperors and Renaissance aristocrats. Its famed villas, gardens and waterworks – both natural and sublimely crafted – make it a worthwhile daytrip.

DISTANCE: 31km (19 miles) east of Rome
TIME: A full day
START: Villa Adriana
END: Villa d'Este
POINTS TO NOTE: Cotral buses to Tivoli leave from Ponte Mammolo (metro line B); bus No. 4 runs from Tivoli's Piazza Garibaldi to Villa Adriana. Trains leave every 20–30 minutes from Tiburtina (metro line B). Not all are direct, and Tivoli's train station is 2km (1.25 miles) from the city centre; local buses connect the two. The time for the last train back to Rome changes but is usually between 9.45pm and 10.30pm. By car you can take the Via Tibertina (SS5) or the slightly quicker (toll) autostrada A24 Roma–L'Aquila (exit Tivoli). Bring a bottle of water with you and wear comfortable walking shoes.

Tivoli lies at the foot of the Tiburtine Hills, in a tuff (porous rock formed from volcanic ash) and sulphur-rich area, where thermal waters create travertine, Rome's signature stone.

Tivoli has long served as a getaway for Romans in the hot summer months. The town itself is rather unremarkable, but its villas and gardens are glorious. The helpful and efficient Tourist Information Office (tel: 0774-313536) in Tivoli is on Piazza Garibaldi, near the COTRAL bus stop.

Tibur

Founded in 1215 BC by Sabine and Latin populations, Classical Tibur (now Tivoli) was an important pre-Roman urban settlement. The city's importance increased with the rise of the Roman Empire, mainly due to its strategic position en route from Rome to the Apennines – the latter being home to Rome's enemy neighbours, the Volsci.

Tivoli was eventually annexed to the empire, with its residents acquiring Roman citizenship in 90 BC. It fast became a popular resort area, as Roman consuls flocked to its mineral-rich thermal waters and built magnificent tuff and travertine villas nearby. Under Emperor Hadrian (117–138), whose villa is now the city's big-

Villa d'Este panoramic views   *Villa d'Este fountains*

gest attraction, the town enjoyed a Golden Age.

Renaissance opulence

In 1461 the Renaissance trend to embellish urban spaces brought Pope Pius II to commission his massive Rocca Pia fortress here. Less than a century later, Cardinal Ippolito d'Este ordered the construction of Villa d'Este, a Baroque gem intended to amaze the visitor with its innumerable *jeux d'eau* (playful fountains). In 1826 Pope Gregory XVI built his Villa Gregoriana in a steep wooded park, set in a rocky gorge. From its galleries, terraces and belvederes, visitors can admire the nearby Grande Cascata (Great Waterfall), fed by the Aniene river, and nearby grottoes.

VILLA ADRIANA

From Tivoli's Piazza Garibaldi you can take bus No. 4 to **Villa Adriana ❶** (Hadrian's Villa; tel: 0774-530 203;

www.villaadriana.beniculturali.it; daily 9am–5.30pm), the largest villa ever to have belonged to a Roman emperor and the most magnificent residence of Imperial times. A Unesco World Heritage Site since 1999, the complex was designed by Hadrian himself. The extensive park, with olive groves and cypresses, houses several buildings inspired by the emperor's journeys to Greece and Egypt.

Inside the grounds

From the ticket office, walk up the road to the **Pecile**, a large pool that was once surrounded by a portico. This is a reproduction of the Stoa Poikile (Painted Porch or Colonnade) that Hadrian had seen in Athens, his favourite city.

East of the Pecile is the **Teatro Marittimo**, believed to be Hadrian's first residence inside the park. The circular vaulted portico with Ionic columns overlooks a canal with a small island in the centre. In Hadrian's time, the only way to get to the island was via a wooden bridge,

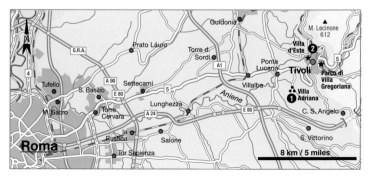

Villa Gregoriana waterfall

which could be removed; on the island was a miniature villa, where the emperor could relax in relative safety and privacy.

Walk south to the **Quartiere Invernale** (Winter Palace), a three-storey complex with a now-empty rectangular fish pond. The traces of a rudimentary heating system suggest that this may have been the emperor's winter residence. Its large banquet hall overlooks distant Rome.

Continue southwards towards the thermal baths. The richly decorated **Piccole Terme** (Small Baths) were reserved for family and important guests, while the **Grandi Terme** (Large Baths) were used by the staff.

In the valley underneath is the **Canopus**, a 119m (390ft) -long strip of water decorated with caryatids. It is named after the ancient Egyptian city that was connected by canal to Alexandria and known for its temple to Serapis. Sculptures from the Canopus are now housed in the Vatican Museums.

At the south end of the Canopus there was a pool house (Serapeum) for entertaining; now all that remains is a large niche in the rock and a chunk of rock in the water basin.

Exit the villa, and catch a local bus back to Piazza Garibaldi in town.

FOOD IN TIVOLI

From Piazza Garibaldi, a 10-minute walk east towards the river will take you to restaurant **L'Angolino di Mirko**, see ❶, a good lunch option. For a dinner on the go, try the famous **Da Pippo**, which makes delicious sandwiches, see ❷.

Before heading to Villa d'Este, stroll along Via della Sibilla (in the northeastern corner of town) where you'll see the round Republican-era **Tempio di Vesta** and the rectangular **Tempio della Sibilla**, dating from 2 AD.

VILLA D'ESTE

Zigzag your way through the medieval streets back towards Piazza Garibaldi and head north on Via Boselli until you reach **Villa d'Este** ❷ (Piazza Trento 5, tel: 0774-332920; www.villadestetivoli.info; daily 8.30am–1 hour before sunset). Originally a Benedictine convent, the villa was converted into the Governor's Palace in the

Villa Gregoriana

Near Tivoli's Temple of Vesta is the entrance to Parco di Villa Gregoriana (Piazza Tempio di Vesta; tel: 0774-332 650; www.villagregoriana.eu; daily 10am–5.30pm, times vary seasonally). The gardens were commissioned by Pope Gregory in 1826 following flooding of the Aniene. To avert future floods the Papal government diverted the river's course, which resulted in a breathtaking 120m (400ft) -high waterfall in the hills. The former riverbed left grottoes and rock formations, which, with the cascade, provide a fine backdrop for the Temple of Vesta and other archaeological finds.

Display at Villa d'Este *Villa d'Este has about 500 fountains*

13th century. In 1550, Cardinal Ippolito d'Este, son of Lucrezia Borgia and grandson of Pope Alexander VI, was elected governor. He immediately set about renovating the villa and its gardens, to turn it into something befitting his aspirations to the papacy. Ippolito commissioned architect and garden designer Pirro Ligorio to design the grounds. Ligorio, who had studied the nearby Villa Adriana, excavated the hillside, laid it out in terraces and built an aqueduct and underground canal fed by the Aniene to supply the extensive waterworks. The gardens took seven years to complete, and their beauty and ingenuity created the desired impact.

The gardens

The villa itself is worth a visit, with its beautiful frescoes, but the main reason the majority of people come here is to see the gardens' wonderful fountains and waterworks. The gardens are laid out, in typical Italian style, on four sweeping terraces, the first of which offers soul-stirring views. Water is diverted from the Aniene river for the Villa d'Este's some 500 fountains; it is a feat of hydraulics ingenious by today's standards, let alone those of the 16th century.

Head down to the second level for **Diana's Grotto** and the **Fontana del Bicchierone** (Fountain of the Great Cup) by Bernini. Go down the staircase on the left for the intricate **Fontana della Rometta**, a miniature representation of Rome landmarks, and, from here, walk behind the **Nymphaeum** (Corridor of the Nymphs)

cascade. This brings you to the **Viale delle Cento Fontane** (Avenue of a Hundred Fountains), a row of pipes that spray water into the air, and the impressive **Fontana dell'Ovato** (Oval Fountain), decorated with nymphs.

Further down still is the central **Fontana dei Draghi** (Fountain of the Dragons), made in honour of Pope Gregory XIII, who was once a guest here, and whose papal insignia included a dragon, and, finally, the 400-year-old **Fontana dell'Organo Idraulico**, with an elaborate water-operated organ that still works.

Food and drink

❶ L'ANGOLINO DI MIRKO

Via della Missione 3; tel: 0774-312027; www.angolinodimirko.com; Tue–Sat 11am–11pm, Sun 10am–4pm; €€€

This elegant restaurant serves traditional food made with high quality ingredients grown on the family farm or bought daily from the Tivoli market. Specialties include handmade pasta, fettuccine with porcini mushrooms, and artichoke pie with cream cheese.

❷ DA PIPPO

Via San Valerio 2; Wed–Mon from 10.30pm; €

Pippo's large sandwiches are so famous that Romans allegedly come all the way to Tivoli for them. Each sandwich is made with up to ten ingredients, and the menu is varied and changes seasonally.

Nemi

CASTELLI ROMANI

Under an hour's drive southeast of Rome will transport you to medieval villages, verdant gardens, the Pope's summer residence and a pagan shrine to the goddess Diana. There's plenty to eat and drink along the way, so take your time and bring your appetite.

DISTANCE: Frascati is 21km (13 miles) southeast of Rome
TIME: At least a full day
START: Frascati
END: Nemi
POINTS TO NOTE: This route requires a car, but all towns mentioned are accessible by train (www.trenitalia.it) or COTRAL bus services, which depart from the car park at Anagnina station at the end of metro line A. If you plan to see the Papal Palace in the morning, drive straight through Frascati and head to Castel Gandolfo as your first stop. For information on sights in the area, contact the Frascati Point (Piazza Marconi, 5; tel: 06-9418 4409; daily 10am–7pm).

In the Alban Hills southeast of Rome, the 13 towns known as the Castelli Romani all grew up around feudal castles and have seen the coming and going of Rome's rich and powerful retreating from the urban chaos. Today they are renowned for their excellent food and wine, and local character.

FRASCATI

The nearest, most famous, of the Castelli, **Frascati ❶** is home to fine villas and gardens, a namesake wine and a breathtaking panorama of Rome. To get here, take the Tuscolana exit from the GRA ring road onto road No. 215, and look out for signs to the town.

Start the day in one of the cafés off Frascati's **Piazza Roma**, then cruise the shops and market square at **Via Regina Margherita** (about a 15-minute walk through the medieval streets).

Villa Aldobrandini

Walk or drive 1.5km (1 mile) southeast of town to **Villa Aldobrandini** (Via **Cardinal** Massaia 18; tel: 06-683 3785; www.aldobrandini.it; gardens: Mon–Fri 9am–1pm and 3–6pm, winters until 5pm; interiors by appointment only). This 17th-century Baroque villa is still occupied by the Aldobrandini family, who rent it out for events, but you can visit the Renaissance gardens. The terraced facade overlooks the city, and the view is perhaps the best panorama in Lazio: it is known as **La Terrazza**

Villa Aldobrandi, Frascati   *Castle Gandolfo*

su Roma (the terrace of Rome).

For lunch at this point, try **Cacciani**, see ❶ (off Piazza Roma back in Frascati).

On leaving, take the SS218 towards Castel Gandolfo, which becomes the SS216; Marino is a turn off to the right.

MARINO

Also known as la Città del Vino (city of wine), **Marino** ❷ gives Frascati wine a run for its money. On the first Sunday of October, it hosts the Sagra dell'Uva, a celebration of the grape harvest. For about an hour the fountain at **Piazza Matteotti** spouts wine instead of water. For lunch here, visit **For de Porta**, see ❷, in Piazza Garibaldi.

Directly across Corso Trieste is the Baroque **Basilica San Barnaba** (Piazza San Barnaba), which houses works of art including a statue of St. Marino overlooking the altar.

ROCCA DI PAPA

The town of **Rocca di Papa** ❸ (The Pope's Rock) lies a few kilometres east of Marino, on the northern flank of the Monte Cavo, the highest peak of the Alban Hills (950m/3,120ft). This pretty medieval town has a *quartiere bavarese*,

named after the Bavarian mercenaries stationed here by Emperor Ludwig III in the 1320s.

CASTEL GANDOLFO

When arriving from the north (from Frascati or Marino), take the SS216 (Via Bruno Buozzi) for **Castel Gandolfo** ❹. In keeping with 400 years of tradition, the Pope spends his summers here at a luxurious palace overlooking **Lago Albano**. The lake is a popular spot for boating and swimming.

Take Via Palazzo Pontificio to reach Bernini's **Residenza Papale**. The palace

Flower festival (infiorata), Genzano

interior can only be visited with special permission. Catch the Sunday Angelus (devotion) in the Piazza della Libertà, near the entrance to the palace, at noon in summer. If there is a Wednesday papal audience it will start around 10am and requires a reservation.

GENZANO

If you're travelling in early to mid-June, stop at the medieval town of **Genzano** 5 for its *infiorata* (flower festival; www.infiorata.it). For three days, residents and guest artists adorn Via Livia (leading from central Piazza IV Novembre to Santa Maria della Cima) with mosaics made of flowers.

Food and drink

1 CACCIANI

Via A. Diaz 13, Frascati; tel: 06-942 0378; www.cacciani.it; Tue–Sat lunch and dinner, Sun lunch only; €€€
This hotel restaurant offers gorgeous views from its terrace and creative regional food. Reservations recommended.

2 FOR DE PORTA

Piazza Garibaldi 18, Marino; tel: 06-938 6783; www.fordeporta.it; Tue–Sun noon–3pm and 6–11pm; €
Order a cheese-and-meat platter or sample some porchetta accompanied by good local wine and enjoy the old feel of this simple *fraschetta*.

NEMI

If coming from Frascati or Castel Gandolfo, take **Via dei Laghi** up and around Lago Albano; it is a gorgeous drive. From Genzano you'll head round the southeastern edge of Lago di Nemi on curvy local roads for 4km (2.5 miles).

The most peaceful of the Castelli villages, in pre-Christian times **Nemi** 6 was the site of an ancient shrine to Diana, goddess of the hunt, and one of Rome's most vociferous cults. Ruins of the ancient temple can be seen on the slopes between the village and the lake.

Evidence of enthusiastic pagan worship was also discovered at the depths of the lake, where Emperor Caligula constructed immense barges for floating ceremonies to the Egyptian goddess Isis. They were first discovered during the Renaissance, but not fully recovered until the 1930s, under Mussolini. The lake was drained, and two ships measuring more than 70m (200ft) long and 20m (65ft) wide were revealed; they were, however, destroyed towards the end of World War II.

Replicas were put in the lakeside **Museo delle Navi Romane di Nemi** (Via del Tempio di Diana 13–15; Mon–Sun 9am–7pm). The museum is 3km (2 miles) from the village of Nemi. Take Corso Vittorio Emanuele to Via Garibaldi; a right turn on to Via Plebiscito will bring you to Via del Tempio di Diana.

To return to Rome, rejoin the SS7 (Via Appia) and head back to the GRA or follow the blue road signs for 'Roma'.

Baths of Neptune, Ostia Antica

OSTIA ANTICA

Long overshadowed by the ruins of the resort-town of Pompeii, the port city of Ostia Antica is an easy day trip from Rome and provides a marvellous picture of ancient Roman life. A 30-minute train ride gets you there, and the nearby beach allows for some leisure time after exploring.

DISTANCE: Ostia Antica is 25km (15 miles) southwest of Rome
TIME: A full day
START: Ostia Antica
END: Lido di Ostia
POINTS TO NOTE: Overground metro trains depart daily from Piramide (metro line B). Alight at Ostia Antica – the ruins are just across the highway bridge. After Ostia Antica take the train back to Rome (direction: Porta San Paolo), or continue to the beaches and restaurants at Lido di Ostia Centro and the next few stops. Ostia Antica is closed on Mondays. Purchase the one-day (*giornaliero*) pass for €6. It's valid until midnight, and allows unlimited rides on the metro, buses and Roma–Ostia train line.

served of all ancient Roman cities, but it also offers a look at varying periods and styles of Roman city life.

The earliest town wall went up in 335 BC, with the sea protecting the settlement at the western side. After nearly 600 years as a bustling port city, Ostia saw a decline during the 4th century AD, suffered a Barbarian sacking 100 years later and was slowly buried under silt and sand, forgotten for centuries.

Sitting at the mouth of the Tiber, Ostia was the first landing point for all the treasures bound for Rome from the far-flung corners of the empire. The shipping business was especially lucrative, and remnants of several luxurious homes are visible at the archaeological site. Maps are available for sale, and, given how much there is to see, it's recommended that you buy one.

OSTIA ANTICA

Ostia Antica (717 Viale dei Romagnoli; www.ostiaantica.beniculturali.it; Tue–Sun 8.30am–6.15pm, until 4pm in winter) is not only one of the best pre-

Decumanus Maximus

Enter the park, pass under the **Porta Romana** city gates and go down the main street, **Decumanus Maximus**, which once linked Ostia to Rome. To the right are the **Terme dei Cisiarii**

Ostia Antica theatre

(Baths of the Coachmen), named after a mosaic.

Baths of Neptune

Stay on the main road and you will pass the foundations of shops and offices. Look for ancient tavern counters and the remains of a bakery's stone ovens; a mosaic of a fish indicates what was sold in one store. Further ahead on the right is a bath complex, the **Terme di Nettuno ❶** (Baths of Neptune), behind a row of shops. Elaborate mosaics depict Neptune and his wife Amphitrite among sea creatures.

Back on the main road, there are remnants of an inscription that once read: FORTVNATVS VINUM E CRATERA QVOD SITIS BIBE or 'Fortunus says to drink wine from the vessel because you are thirsty.'

Theatre

Next you will encounter the large, heavily restored **Teatro ❷** (theatre), with 3,000 seats. Built under Agrippa, in the 1st century BC, it was enlarged a century later. The orchestra was originally covered in marble and was flooded for small-scale sea scenes. Keep an eye out for small shrines; many Christians were executed in the theatre.

Behind the theatre, the big shippers and traders had their offices in the **Piazzale delle Corporazioni** (Square of the Guilds). There were at least 60 of these offices, and it's worth seeing their ancient 'trademarks' and the mosaics depicting scenes of city life. The River Tiber ran by the piazza in those days (it has since slightly changed its course).

Forum

Continuing on the main road, on the left is the former laundry service. Turn right for the excavation **museum**, café and toilets, otherwise continue straight ahead and take the road for the **Capitolium** Curia, which stands at one end of the **Foro ❸** (Forum). This temple to the Capitoline triad (Jupiter, Juna and

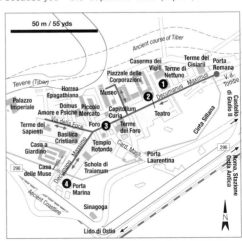

Mosaic, Baths of Neptune

Ostia Antica's main street

Minerva) has steps as impressive as those in any modern capital city.

On the other side of the forum is the **Tempio Rotondo**, dedicated to deified emperors. Less distinguishable are the remains of a courthouse *(curia)*, city council and a basilica. Further along is a round temple, dedicated to the deified emperors of Rome.

After you exit the forum you will reach a fork. **Decumano Massimo** veers slightly left toward the **Porta Marina ❹**, the ancient coastline, where a synagogue dating back to the 1st century BC was recently uncovered. You'll pass an expansive house and garden structure in Hadrianesque grandeur.

Return to the fork. **Via della Foce** veers right toward **Domus Amore e Psiche**, named after a statue of Cupid and Psyche found on the premises. Marble and granite columns support pretty arches, and there's a tiny courtyard beyond. Further up the street are more bathhouses and a granary.

Medieval castle

On your way back to the train station, turn down Piazzale della Rocca from Viale dei Romagnoli, and you will see the **Castello di Giulio II**, built in 1483 by Baccio Pontelli and viewed as one of the best examples of Renaissance fortification; also here is the medieval town of Ostia. The castle was constructed as a papal apartment and is now a small museum. The frescoes on the main staircase are by Baldassare Peruzzi. Phone ahead to visit the castle (tel: 06-5635 8013; visits: Sat–Sun 9.30am–6.30pm).

LIDO DI OSTIA

If you plan on soaking up some sun before dinner, reserve a table in advance at **La Vecchia Pineta**, see ❶, and take the train to **Castel Fusano**. The beach club and restaurant are directly in front of you. Lounge chairs and umbrellas are available for rent. Sandwiches and ice creams are available at the bar on site.

Another option is to get off at the previous stops of **Ostia Centro** or **Stella Polare** and head to the beachfront avenue, where you can grab a slice of pizza or fresh seafood. This area is packed with beach clubs (many free).

Note that trains back to Rome stop running around 11pm.

Food and drink

❶ LA VECCHIA PINETA

Piazza dell'Aquilone 4 (Lungomare Lutazio Catulo); tel: 06-5647 0282; www. lavecchiapineta.com; daily lunch and dinner; €€

A seafront setting adds to the appeal of this seafood restaurant. Try *spaghetti allo scoglio*, a spicy clam sauce, and fried *(fritto misto)* or grilled *(grigliata mista)* mixed seafood platters.

DIRECTORY

Hand-picked hotels and restaurants to suit all budgets and tastes, organised by area, plus select nightlife listings, an alphabetical listing of practical information, a language guide and an overview of the best books and films to give you a flavour of the city.

Looking towards the Hotel 47

ACCOMMODATION

Traditionally Rome has always been an expensive city to stay in, with price often a poor reflection of quality. In recent years the accommodation options have begun to broaden, so that, while most hotels are still expensive, you can now choose to avoid the peeling pensione of old. Conventional facades now hide avant-garde interiors, while at the grander end of the scale, gracious, timeless hotels retain their cachet. But for those not on an imperial budget, there are plenty of welcoming guesthouses and family-run hotels, while self-catering apartments, bed and breakfasts and Airbnb are increasingly popular options.

In terms of location, the area around Piazza Navona, the Pantheon, and Campo de' Fiori offers perhaps the best introduction to the city, since you are right in its medieval heart and within easy reach of most main sights. However, there are relatively few hotels in the area, and these tend to be booked up early, so try to plan ahead if possible.

> Prices for an average double room in high season:
> €€€€ = €350 and above
> €€€ = €180–350
> €€ = €100–180
> € = under €100

The Forum and Colosseum

Capo d'Africa
Via Capo d'Africa 54; tel: 06-772 801; www.hotelcapodafrica.com; metro: Colosseo; €€€
This hotel's dramatic, palm-tree-lined entrance bodes well, and its rooms are comfortable and contemporary. Views are delightful, especially from the glass-walled rooftop breakfast room.

Domus Sessoriana
Piazza Santa Croce in Gerusalemme 10; tel: 06-706 151; www.domussessoriana.it; metro: Lodi; €€
Attached to the monastery of the church next door, this hotel offers simple, elegant accommodation. Request a room overlooking the monastery's garden.

Forum
Via Tor de' Conti 25–30; tel: 06-679 2446; www.hotelforum.com; metro: Cavour or Colosseo; €€€€
This luxurious, oldfashioned hotel is ideally located for the Forum, with a wonderful view from its roof-garden restaurant.

Hotel 47
Via Petroselli 47; tel: 06-678 7816; www.fortysevenhotel.com; bus: 30, 44, 81, 83, 85, 170 €€€€
This plush modern hotel is set in an austere 1930s building that has been

Hotel 47 interior   *Hotel 47's rooftop restaurant*

tastefully converted and filled with repro furniture and contemporary artworks. The views are wonderful, especially from the rooftop restaurant.

Inn at the Roman Forum
Via degli Ibernesi 30; tel: 06-6919 0970; www.theinnattheromanforum.com; bus: 40, 75 Metro: Colosseo; €€€€
This boutique hotel offers luxurious rooms with canopied beds, antique furnishings, a prime location and even its own ancient Roman crypt.

Trevi Fountain and Quirinale
DaphneTrevi
Via degli Avignonesi 20, Trevi; tel: 06-8953 8471; www.daphne-rome.com; metro: Barberini; €€
This hotel offers excellent service with friendly staff, Wi-Fi connection and charming interiors.

Residenza Cellini
Via Modena 5; tel: 06-4782 5204; www.residenzacellini.it; metro: Repubblica; €€€
With rooms that are unusually large for the price, this hotel is deservedly popular. The decor is classic, with parquet floors, wood furnishings and fabrics in flouncy florals.

Piazza di Spagna and Tridente
Gregoriana
Via Gregoriana 18; tel: 06-679 4269; www.hotelgregoriana.it; metro: Spagna or Barberini; €€

Fans of Art Deco will adore the striking retro interior of this ex-convent, with its wonderful lift and original 1930s room numbers by the Russian fashion designer Erté.

Hassler
Piazza Trinità dei Monti 6; tel: 06-699 340; www.hotelhasslerroma.com; metro: Spagna; €€€€
Situated above the Spanish Steps, this historic establishment is still one of Rome's most alluring luxury hotels, its olde-worlde glamour a real contrast with the sleek minimalism of some of the city's new five-stars. The restaurant, with roof gardens and views over the city, is particularly beautiful.

Hotel Art
Via Margutta 56; tel: 06-328 711; www.hotelart.it; metro: Spagna; €€€€
Set in a converted seminary, this upmarket hotel blends old and new. The reception area is within two futuristic pods, while the sleek lounge area is beneath frescoed vaulted ceilings.

Hotel Panda
Via della Croce 35; tel: 06-678 0179; www.hotelpanda.it; metro: Spagna; €
A rare budget option a stone's throw from the Spanish Steps, Panda's rooms, though small and pretty basic, have been attractively decorated, and some have wood-beamed ceilings. Book early.

Bath with a view at the Hassler

Inn at the Spanish Steps
Via dei Condotti 85; tel: 06-6992 5657; www.atspanishsteps.com; metro: Spagna; €€€€

The stunning rooms at this luxury boutique hotel are a mix of carefully selected antiques and bold fabrics; some boast 17th-century frescoes, others have views directly over the Spanish Steps. A sister hotel, the View at the Spanish Steps, along the same road at No. 91, is similarly luxurious, though slightly more pared-down in style.

Modigliani
Via della Purificazione 42; tel: 06-4281 5226; www.hotelmodigliani.com; metro: Spagna; €€

A lovely hotel with great views from top-floor rooms and a garden in an inner courtyard.

Portrait Roma
Via Bocca di Leone, 23; tel: 06-6938 0742; www.lungarnocollection.com/portrait-roma; metro: Spagna; €€€€

Winner of the Forbes five star award for three consecutive years, this hotel offers contemporary Italian luxury and stunning views.

Royal Suite Trinità dei Monti
Piazza di Spagna 29; tel: 06-8352 1675; www.suitetrinitadeimonti.com; metro: Spagna; €€€

Directly accessible from the Spanish Steps. This boutique hotel offers traditional style rooms, some with incredible balconies and small terraces.

Scalinata di Spagna
Piazza Trinità dei Monti 17; tel: 06-4568 6150; www.hotelscalinata.com; metro: Spagna; €€€

A small hotel in a beautiful town house at the top of the Spanish Steps. Breakfast can be taken on a rooftop terrace in summer. Book early.

The Vatican and Prati

Bramante
Vicolo delle Palline 24; tel: 06-6880 6426; www.hotelbramante.com; metro: Ottaviano; €€€

This 15th-century former inn on a tranquil side street near St Peter's is now a charming hotel. The small terrace makes a pleasant place to unwind after a busy day.

Colors
Via Boezio 31; tel: 06-687 4030; www.colorshotel.com; metro: Ottaviano; €€

A bright, clean budget (two-star) hotel, which offers contemporarily decorated, wonderfully lofty rooms with or without en suite bathroom, and dormitory accommodation. Has several family rooms, too. Fabulous value for money. Kitchen, laundry facilities and a roof terrace.

Farnese
Via Alessandro Farnese 30; tel: 06-321 2553; www.hotelfarnese.com; bus: 30, 87; metro: Lepanto; €€€

This upmarket four-star hotel occupies a grand old aristocratic residence. The attention to detail and period furnish-

Funky Hassler suite

Breakfast at Inn at the Spanish Steps

ings are what make it so special. Rooms are elegant with antiques, marble bathrooms and Murano lamps. The breakfast is excellent, and there is a pretty roof terrace. The hotel is within walking distance of St Peter's.

Franklin

Via Rodi 29; tel: 06-3903 0165; www. franklinhotelrome.it; metro: Ottaviano; €€€
This unique, modern hotel has airy, pleasant rooms, all with a musical theme. There are Bang Olufsen audio systems in every room and an extensive music collection for guests to borrow from. You can also borrow bicycles, should you wish to explore the Vatican on two wheels.

Rome Cavalieri

Via Alberto Cadlolo 101; tel: 06-35091; www.romecavalieri.it; Metro: Barbereni to Via Veneto and the Rome Cavalieri Shuttle Bus; €€€€
Luxury hotel of the Waldorf Astoria group situated on top of Monte Mario, just north of the Vatican. It is quiet and spacious, and offers amenities that more central hotels lack – tennis courts and indoor and outdoor swimming pools among them – as well as one of Rome's best restaurants (La Pergola) on the top floor, which spreads onto the terrace in summer.

Piazza Navona and the Pantheon

Due Torri

Vicolo del Leonetto 23, off Via dell'Orso;

tel: 06-6880 6956; www.hotelduetorriroma. com; bus: 70, 81, 87; €€
A delightful hotel – in a former cardinal's palace tucked away down a narrow cobbled street – and quiet by Roman standards; those on the top floor have terraces.

Grand Hotel de la Minerve

Piazza della Minerva 69; tel: 06-695 201; www.grandhoteldelaminerve.com; bus: 40, 64, 70; €€€€
Built within a 17th-century palazzo overlooking the lovely Piazza della Minerva. Vast areas of Venetian glass create spectacular public spaces. Rooms are large, and there are splendid views from the roof terrace.

Navona

Via dei Sediari 8; tel: 06-6830 1252; www. hotelnavona.com; bus: 70, 81, 87; €€
This family-run hotel, on the second floor of an attractive palazzo, was built on the site of the ancient baths of Agrippa – the ground floor dates back to AD 1. Good value for the location.

Raphael

Largo Febo 2, off Piazza Navona; tel: 06-682 831; www.raphaelhotel.com; bus: 30, 70, 81, 87; €€€€
A distinctive ivy-covered exterior, antique furnishings, artworks and stunning views. The Richard Meier-designed 'executive' rooms on the third floor are sleek and modern, while the rest of the hotel has a clas-

Grand Hotel de la Minerve

sic feel. Some rooms don't quite live up to expectations but facilities, the rooftop restaurant, bar and the views most certainly do.

Sole al Pantheon
Piazza della Rotonda 63; tel: 06-678 0441; www.hotelsolealpantheon.com; metro: Barberini; €€€€

This 500-year-old hotel, a stone's throw from the Pantheon, has been renovated without spoiling the atmosphere. Front rooms have memorable views but are quite noisy. Quieter rooms overlook an internal courtyard. The decor is serene and fresh, with tiled floors, high ceilings and frescoes.

Teatro Pace 33
Via del Teatro Pace 33; tel: 06-687 9075; www.hotelteatropace.com; bus: 30, 46, 62, 70, 81, 87 ; €€

This 17th-century building on a quiet backstreet has a magnificent Baroque spiral staircase (there's no lift) and wood-beamed rooms decorated in classic style, with marble bathrooms.

Campo de' Fiori and the Ghetto

Campo de' Fiori
Piazza del Biscione 6; tel: 06-6887 4886; www.hotelcampodefiori.com; bus: 64, 70; €€

This hotel has a beautiful roof terrace, intimate, individually decorated rooms with en-suite bathrooms, and common spaces decorated in rich velvets.

Lunetta
Piazza del Paradiso 68; tel: 06-6839 5056; www.hotellunetta.com; bus: 64, 70, 87; Metro: Corso Vittorio Emanuele; €€€€

The building dates from 1368, but the hotel was renovated in 2011, providing the perfect balance of tradition and trendiness. There's a spa, a bar and multiple rooftop gardens, and the location is great, right around the corner from Campo de'Fiori.

Teatro di Pompeo
Largo del Pallaro 8; tel: 06-6830 0170; www.hotelteatrodipompeo.it; bus: 46, 62, 64; €€

This simple, old-fashioned hotel was built on the site of the ancient Theatre of Pompey (the remains can still be seen in the vaulted breakfast room).

Via Veneto and Villa Borghese

Aldrovandi Palace
Via Ulisse Aldrovandi 15; tel: 06-322 3993; www.aldrovandi.com; tram: 2, 3, 19; €€€€

Sumptuous rooms and suites at this beautiful hotel. The lovely gardens, spectacular outdoor pool and restaurant (Baby), run by a Michelin-starred chef, are further draws.

Eden
Via Ludovisi 49; tel: 06-478 121; www.dorchestercollection.com; bus: 52, 53, 61, 63; Metro; Spagna; €€€€

This discreet, ultra-refined hotel rejects ostentatious opulence in favour of

The elegant Grand Hotel de la Minerve

classic, pared-down elegance. Excellent, unsnooty service, and a Michelin-starred roof garden restaurant, La Terrazza dell' Eden, with views to die for.

Lord Byron
Via Giuseppe de Notaris 5; tel: 06-322 0404; www.lordbyronhotel.com; bus: 52; €€€€
Built into a former monastery, this small hotel has the atmosphere of a vintage private club, and enjoys a serene location away from the city centre.

Sofitel Roma Villa Borghese
Via Lombardia 47; tel: 06-478 021; www.sofitel.com; metro: Spagna or Barberini; €€€€
Old-style elegance and traditional service. The rooms are spacious and furnished with character, the staff are professional and friendly, and the rooftop terrace offers a breathtaking view of the whole city.

Westin Excelsior
Via Vittorio Veneto 125; tel: 06-47081; www.marriott.com; metro: Barberini; €€€€
Part of the 1950s dolce vita scene and always the grandest of Via Veneto's five-stars, the Excelsior offers the ultimate in opulence and glamour, with staggeringly luxurious, antiques-laden rooms.

Trastevere and the Gianicolo
Arco del Lauro
Via dell'Arco de' Tolomei 29, off Via del Salumi; tel: 06-9784 0350; www.

arcodellauro.it; tram: 8, bus 23, 280; €€
A four-room B&B, in a tranquil part of Trastevere. Fresh, simple and excellent-value rooms, decorated in simple style. Breakfast is served in a nearby bar.

Relais Casa della Fornarina
Via di Porta Settimiana 7; tel: 06-6456 2268; www.casadellafornarina.com; bus: 23, 280; €€
A modern guesthouse created inside an historic Trastevere house, where Raphael's 'Baker Girl' is said to have lived in the 1500s. Spacious rooms, with wooden ceilings. Italian breakfast is served at the nearby bar.

Residenza Arco dei Tolomei
Via dell'Arco de' Tolomei 27; tel: 06-5832 0819; www.inrome.info; tram: 8, bus 23, 280; €€
On a quiet alley with just five rooms, three with terraces. Decorated in country-house style, with a homely feel. Breakfast is a real event here, with homemade baked goods and jams served in a light-filled breakfast room.

San Francesco
Via Jacopa de' Settesoli 7; tel: 06-5830 0051; www.hotelsanfrancesco.net; bus: 44, 75; Tram 3, 8; €€
Set back from the bustle of central Trastevere, rooms are good-sized and comfortable; ask for one of the rooms overlooking the internal courtyard of the adjacent convent. Breakfast is served on the roof terrace in warm weather.

Aldrovandi Palace pool

Santa Maria

Vicolo del Piede 2; tel: 06-589 4626; www.hotelsantamariatrastevere.it; bus: H, 23; Tram: 8; €€

Gated, refurbished 16th-century cloister. Rooms are large and comfortable, with a view out onto a sunny central courtyard planted with orange trees. Bikes are available for guests' use. One room is disabled-accessible.

Trastevere

Via L. Manara 24A; tel: 06-581 4713; www.hoteltrastevere.net; bus: H; Tram: 8; €€

With clean, simple rooms overlooking Piazza San Cosimato market square, this charming, down-to-earth little hotel is a great deal for the area, with good-value apartments for rent in the vicinity.

Villa della Fonte

Villa della Fonte d'Olio 8; tel: 06-580 3797; www.villafonte.com; bus: H; Tram: 8; €€

In a quiet alley near Santa Maria in Trastevere, this small hotel has a delightful roof garden where guests can enjoy their breakfast. The rooms are simple but furnished with taste, and they are all air-conditioned.

Sant'Anselmo

Piazza Sant'Anselmo 2; tel: 06-570 057; www.aventinohotels.com; metro: Circo Massimo; €€€

Nestling in a peaceful garden on the exclusive Aventine Hill, each room in this hotel has been given its own

imaginative theme. Four-poster beds, free-standing baths and frescoes make it a very special place to stay.

Villa San Pio

Via di Santa Melania 19; tel: 06-570 057; www.aventinohotels.com; metro: Circo Massimo; €€

This hotel consists of three separate buildings that share the same attractive gardens. It has elegant, spacious rooms decked out with antique furnishings as well as generous bathrooms with Jacuzzis.

Montreal

Via Carlo Alberto 4; tel: 06-445 7797; www.hotelmontrealrome.com; metro: Termini, Vittorio Emanuele; €€

The Montreal's 27 rooms are bright, cheery and spacious, and its small, flower-filled patio makes a lovely spot to enjoy breakfast during the summer months.

Palazzo Naiadi, the Dedica Anthology

Piazza della Repubblica 47; tel: 06-489 381; www.marriott.com; metro: Termini; €€€€

Only a few minutes' walk from Rome's Termini station, this hotel is among the most opulent of the city's five-star options. The Palazzo Naiadi is glamorous, with luxurious, no-expense-spared rooms and stunning suites that are a favourite with visiting film stars.

Reception at the Eden   Suite at the Eden

Radisson Blu es. Hotel

Via Filippo Turati 171; tel: 06-444 841;
www.rezidor.com; metro: Termini, Vittorio
Emanuele; €€€

This cutting-edge-design hotel has a
spectacular rooftop terrace with a restaurant and a pool (in summer). Its location opposite the station is convenient
but far from picturesque.

La Villa Del Patrizio

Via Di Castelfusano 21; tel: 06-565 0960; €€
Offers simple but clean, airy rooms only
500m from the train station which provides easy access to Rome's city centre and the Ostia Lido beach. The Ostia
Antica archaeological ruins are just
2km away.

Tivoli

Grand Hotel Duca D'Este

Via Tiburtina Valeria 330; tel: 0774-3883;
www.ducadeste.com; €€€

The nearby thermal centre is the main
attraction at this high-profile hotel complex. Designed for large groups, Duca
D'Este offers spa services for a relaxing stay. There's a covered pool and an
outdoor pool in the garden, as well as a
sauna and massage room.

Palazzo Maggiore

Via Giuliani 89; tel: 393 104 4937; www.
palazzomaggiore.com; €

Housed in a palazzo from the 1700s,
this B&B is artfully decorated with colourful fabrics and tasteful furnishings.

A fabulous breakfast is served on the
delightful terrace or in the owner's
kitchen. In a perfect location right in the
historic centre of Tivoli.

Castelli Romani

Grand Hotel Villa Tuscolana

Via del Tuscolo km 1.5, Frascati; tel: 06-942
900; www.villatuscolana.it; €€€

Just east of Frascati, this beautiful hillside villa has been lavishly restored
and turned into a hotel with 110 rooms.
The bedrooms are spacious and elegant, and the common areas – which
include a restaurant (La Rufinella) and
bar – impressively grand. It also has an
indoor pool.

Hotel Flora

Viale Vittorio Veneto 8, Frascati; tel: 06-941
6110; www.hotel-flora.it; €€

The bright bedrooms and luxurious
marble bathrooms at this hotel, built
in the late 19th century and decorated
in Art Nouveau ('Liberty') style, make it
an appealing option if you're looking to
stay in central Frascati. There's a pretty
courtyard shaded by palm trees where
you can take breakfast in warm weather.

Park Hotel Villa Grazioli

Via Umberto Pavoni 19, Grottaferrata; tel:
06-945 500; www.villagrazioli.com; €€

This four-star hotel offers elegant rooms
inside the grand palace façade. Mature
trees punctuate the grounds creating
a secluded ambience and there is an
amazing outdoor swimming pool.

Dining alfresco in Trastevere

RESTAURANTS

Rome has some excellent restaurants worth seeking out, though not for local fare – few consider la *cucina romana* the best of Italy's regional cuisines – but Rome may well be one of Italy's most pleasurable cities in which to eat. Most restaurants plan on one seating per evening, so you will not be rushed, or pressured to leave. Often, what might seem to be slow service is merely the Roman way of stretching a meal far into the night. When in Rome, enjoy *la dolce vita* with a long, lingering meal – and have it in the open air, if the weather is good. Remember that many *enoteche* (wine bars) have full menus too.

The Forum and Colosseum

Gelateria Vacanze Romane
Piazza Ara Coeli 10; tel: 06-6477 0044; daily 10am–8pm; €
This is a great gelateria just near the steps to the Capitoline Hill. In addition to their homemade gelato (including the deepest, darkest chocolate fondant), they also have sugarless, gluten-free and milk-free versions.

Price guide for a two-course meal for one with half a bottle of house wine.
€€€€ = €60 and above
€€€ = €40–60
€€ = €25–40
€ = under €25

Hostaria Nerone
Via delle Terme di Tito 96; tel: 06-481 7952; Mon–Sat noon–3pm and 7–11pm; €€
A classic osteria that serves up great home cooking, with views overlooking the Colosseum. Their antipasto, oxtail stew and veal are all excellent. The best choice for atmosphere and quality in the area.

Pane & Vino
Via Ostilia 10; tel: 06-7720 7177; daily 10am–4.30pm; €
This small and cosy sandwich shop, which uses fresh ingredients, is perfect for those looking for a quick bite. The super veg sandwich is particularly good. Gluten free options are available.

Ristorante Cleto
Via del Buon Consiglio 17; tel: 06-6994 1507; www.ristorantecleto.it; daily noon–11.30pm; €€
This family-style *ristorante* is a good choice for a relaxed lunch or dinner on a side street away from the dust and crowds of the Colosseum. They have a wonderful antipasto bar and make a memorable fish ravioli.

Ristorante Mario's
Piazza del Grillo 5; tel: 06-679 3725; Tue–Sun 12.30–3.30pm, 7.30–11pm; €€
Traditional Roman food served (fish is their speciality) at surprisingly affordable prices in this touristy area. Informal

Understated elegance in a Roman restaurant

at lunchtimes, more elegant for dinner; lovely pergola in the square outside.

Trevi Fountain and Quirinale

Al Moro

Vicolo delle Bollette 13; tel: 06-678 3495; www.ristorantealmororoma.it; Mon–Sat 12.30–3.30pm and 7.30–11.30pm; €€€
Located just a few minutes from the Trevi Fountain is this old favourite with the local boutique owners and Via dei Condotti shoppers. The menu is classic, with Roman pastas and artichokes, but with a twist – also featuring Sicilian fish dishes such as swordfish and calamari, and fish carpaccio.

Le Colline Emiliane

Via degli Avignonesi 22; tel: 06-481 7538; www.collineemiliane.com; Tue–Sat 12.45–2.45pm and 7.30–10.45pm, Sun 12.45–2.45pm; €€€
This lovely restaurant, which is situated just near the Palazzo Barberini, serves up mouthwatering dishes from the Emilia-Romagna region. Their northern-style sauces and stewed or grilled meats are a wonderful change to typical, ubiquitous pasta dishes.

Il Gelato di San Crispino

Via della Panetteria 42; tel: 06-679 3924; www.ilgelatodisancrispino.com; daily 11am–12.30am, Fri–Sat until 1.30am; €
The handmade gelato served here – in paper cups rather than cones, which are said to contaminate the flavour – is thought by some to be the best in the country, let alone the city. Be sure to try the honey-flavoured San Crispino, sesame or dark chocolate.

Piccolo Arancio

Vicolo Scanderbeg 112; tel: 06-678 6139; www.piccoloarancio.it; Tue–Sun noon–3pm, 6.30pm–midnight; €€
Sit for lunch or dinner at this restaurant's charming outdoor tables just behind the Quirinale, and order speciality dishes such as ravioli with an orange and ricotta filling, or creamy risotto with radicchio.

Vineria Il Chianti

Via del Lavatore 81; tel: 06-679 2470; www.vineriailchianti.com; daily 12.30–3.30pm, 7–11.20pm; €€
Just around the corner from the Trevi Fountain is this cute Tuscan wine bar with decent food. They serve Florentine steaks and pasta with a wild boar sauce, plus a great selection of Chianti.

Piazza di Spagna and Tridente

Al 34

Via Mario dei Fiori 34; tel: 06-679 5091; www.ristoranteal34.it; Tue–Sun 12.30–11pm, Mon 5.30–11pm; €€
The service is fast, the prices honest, the atmosphere lively and the food classical Italian. Sample the *tonnarelli al granciporro* (pasta with crab), the fresh fish *misto* (a mix of different fish), the homemade Neapolitan *torta caprese*, *semifreddo al torronocino* (nougat ice cream dessert) or the pear and chocolate tart.

La Cicala e la Formica

Babette

Via Margutta 1b; tel: 06-321 1559; www.
babetteristorante.it; Tue–Sat 1–3pm and
7–10.30pm; €€

The atmosphere is that of a French bras-
serie from the early 1900s, but the cuisine is decidedly Italian, with traditional
flavours and many new inventions from
the chef. Breakfast is especially pleasant,
with hot croissants and bread with jam.
There's a buffet at lunchtime and menu à
la carte in the evening. The outdoor tables
spill out on the lovely piazzetta, but they
go fast, so book ahead.

Dal Bolognese

Piazza del Popolo 1; tel: 06-322 2799; https://
roma.dalbolognese.it; daily 12.45–3pm,
8.15–11pm; €€€

This classic restaurant is elegant but not
stuffy and has returning clientele that
include celebrities and models. The menu
is also traditional with – unsurprisingly –
favourites such as *pasta Bolognese* and
a tortellini soup. They serve an excellent
selection of shellfish dishes, and expensive but good wines.

Il Gabriello

Via Vittorla 51; tol: 06-6994 0810; www.
ilgabriello.com; Mon–Sat 7–11pm; €€

Though Il Gabriello is below street level
(it's the former wine cellar of a 17th-cen-
tury palazzo), the setting is truly beautiful, with vaulted ceilings and the perfect
lighting – only the music is sometimes a
bit too loud. The family-run service adds
a touch of home, and the cuisine serves

traditional dishes made with high-quality raw materials. One example: beef fillet
cooked in Brunello di Montalcino, or the
usual *pasta cacio e pepe*.

'Gusto al 28

Piazza Augusto Imperatore 28; tel: 06-6813
4221; www.gusto.it; daily lunch and dinner
daily, Sat, Sun brunch; restaurant €€€,
pizzeria €€

'Gusto is an empire: a pizzeria down-
stairs, an upmarket restaurant upstairs,
a wine bar on the other side, an osteria
next to that. There's even a well-stocked
cookery store attached. The service is
fast and friendly, and the general standard is high. An added feature is the outdoor seating most of the year under
impressively austere 1930s porticoes
that line the square. Booking advisable.
Open late.

Hostaria dell'Orso

Via dei Soldati 25c; tel: 06-6830 1192; www.
hdo.it; Mon–Sat 7.30–11.30pm only; €€€€

Founded by Milanese superstar chef
Gualtiero Marchesi the exclusive Hostaria
dell'Orso is in a palazzo that dates back
to the 1400s. Now a posh but hip restau-
rant-cum-piano bar-cum-disco, it has an
expensive take on Italian haute cuisine
that can be ordered à la carte or from four
different set-price menus.

Life

Via della Vite 28; tel: 06-6938 0948; www.
ristorantelife.it; Tue–Sat noon–midnight, Mon
5pm–midnight; €€€

Alfresco dining　　　　　　　　　　　　　　*Italian pastries*

This restaurant and pizzeria is modern and minimal inside, and comfortable and romantic outside. Colourful art fills the walls and the atmosphere is youthful and relaxed. The bread, pasta and desserts are homemade, plus the menu lists the staples of Roman cuisine as well as a few creative dishes, including both meat and fish recipes prepared with the freshest ingredients.

Il Margutta Vegetarian food & art

Via Margutta 118; tel: 06-3265 0577; www.ilmargutta.bio; daily 9.30am–11.30pm; €€€

A vegetarian's haven in the middle of lamb-loving Rome, where you'll find excellently prepared creative dishes, versions of classic favourites and contemporary art on the wall.

Matricianella

Via del Leone 4; tel: 06-683 2100; www.matricianella.it; Mon–Sat 12.30–3pm and 7.30–11pm; €€

Classic Roman dishes are served in a bustling atmosphere where the decor is akin to an Italian grandmother's kitchen. To start, try their crispy *fritti* (deep fried vegetables, courgette flowers and morsels of meat in batter) and then perhaps the *abbacchio al forno* (roast suckling lamb).

The Vatican and Prati

Benito e Gilberto al Falco

Via del Falco 19; tel: 06-686 7769; www.benitoegilberto.it; Tue–Sat noon–3pm, 7pm–11.30pm; €€€

This is a seafood lover's delight. Nearly every dish is fish-based and only the freshest is served. Photos on the wall testify to the many celebrities who have eaten here.

La Locanda di Pietro

Via Sebastiano Veniero 28/c; tel: 06-8778 4145; www.lalocandadipietro.it/en; daily 11am–3.30pm and 6–11pm; €€€

Chef Roberto Cipolla works to combine traditional flavours with modern touches. The menu changes seasonally so only the freshest, local ingredients can be utilised. The stuffed entrecote with wild mushrooms is a good choice if available.

Il Matriciano

Via dei Gracchi 55; tel: 06-321 2327; www.ilmatriciano.it; Thu–Mon 12.30–3pm and 7.45–11pm, Tue 7.45–11pm; €€

Just around the corner from St Peter's this restaurant has served genuine local food for over 90 years. Its signature dish is an excellent *spaghetti all'amatriciana* (spaghetti with tomato, onion and cured pork sauce).

Napul'è

Viale Giulio Cesare 89–91; tel: 06-323 1005; www.napularte.it; daily noon–3pm and 7pm–midnight; €

Neapolitans approve of the pizza at this southern restaurant. Choose from a wide variety of different styles, all boasting the typical thick crust (as opposed to the thin Roman pizza).

High-end bruschetta

Also serves pasta and meat dishes from the Campania region and offers live music some nights.

Osteria dell'Angelo

Via G. Bettolo 24-32; tel: 06-372 9470; Mon–Fri 12.30–2.30pm and 7.30–11pm, Sat 7.30–11pm; €€

This neighbourhood trattoria with a fixed-price evening menu, including house wine, is always packed to the gills. Try the *fritti* to begin with, then a flavourful version of the Roman standard *tonnarelli cacio e pepe* (pasta with pecorino and pepper). Booking advisable. No credit cards.

La Pergola

Rome Cavalieri, Via A. Cadlolo 101, Monte Mario; tel: 06-3509 2152; https://romecavalieri.com/la-pergola; Tue–Sat 7.30–11.30pm; €€€€

German superstar chef Heinz Beck has made this a place worth making a detour for. Breathtaking views, attentive staff and ultra-refined food. There is a reason that this place has three Michelin stars. Elegant dress code.

Siciliainbocca

Via Faà di Bruno 26; tel: 06-3735 8400; www.siciliainbocca.com; Mon–Sat lunch and dinner, Sun lunch only; €€

Come here for a cheerful ambience and good Sicilian food seasoned with the island's flavours: lemons, olives, capers and plenty of sunshine. Their classic ricotta-filled *cassata* is excellent.

Taverna Angelica

Piazza Capponi 6; tel: 06-687 4514; www.tavernaangelica.com; Fri–Sat 6pm–midnight, Sun 11.30am–3.30pm, 6pm–midnight, Mon–Thu 11.30am–4pm and 6pm–midnight; €€

For the last 20 plus years Taverna Angelica has earned a reputation for high-quality food. Try the octopus with celery, blackberries and green creams; ravioli with spicy salt cod and capers or the seared salmon with mushrooms and asparagus cream.

Trattoria Dal Toscano

Via Germanico 58; tel: 06-3972 5717; Tue–Sun 12.30–3pm, 8–11.15pm; €€

Tuscan specialities are served up in this large, friendly trattoria. Dishes include pappardelle, grilled Florentine steaks and home-baked sweets. Outdoor dining is possible in the summer months.

Piazza Navona and the Pantheon

Al Duello

Via della Vaccarella 11a; tel: 06-687 3348; www.ristorantealduello.com; Sat–Sun noon–3pm, 6.30–11pm, Mon, Wed–Fri 6.30–11pm; €€

Named after the famous duel, in which Caravaggio killed his friend Ranuccio, this welcoming trattoria commemorates the painter's wrongdoings. Service is attentive and friendly, the food is good and the wine selection sophisticated.

Casa Bleve

Via del Teatro Valle 48–49; tel: 06-686 5970;

Courgette flowers   *Fried artichoke*

www.casableve.com; Mon–Sat 12.30–3pm, 7.30–11pm; €€

Set against the backdrop of the restored Palazzo Medici Lante della Rovere. An enormous semicircular counter is laden with all kinds of cold meats, salads and cheeses. Beyond, there's seating in a large, atmospherically lit room. With an exceptional wine list, this is a high-level enoteca worth seeking out. Closed for three weeks in August.

Clemente alla Maddalena

Piazza della Maddalena 4; tel: 06-683 3633; www.clementeallamaddalena.it; daily 12.30–3.30pm, 7–11.30pm; €€€

Clemente alla Maddalena's owner prides himself on the freshness of the ingredients, and the menu changes according to the season, with fresh fish, selected meat cuts, and porcini mushrooms in autumn. The setting is charming and elegant, and there is a pleasant terrace for dining in the summer months too.

Il Convivio Troiani

Vicolo dei Soldati 31; tel: 06-686 9432; www.ilconviviotroiani.it; Mon–Sat 7.30–11pm; €€€€

Run by three brothers, Il Convivio is one of the city's foremost gastronomic temples. Equal emphasis is placed on vegetable, fish and meat options, always prepared with organic ingredients that are combined to create something unexpected. Three elegant rooms and well-trained staff make for a truly rounded gourmet experience.

Cul de Sac

Piazza Pasquino 73; tel: 06-6880 1094; www.enotecaculdesacroma.it; daily noon–12.30am; €€

One of the best-stocked wine bars in Rome, with a Parisian feel. Space may be tight in the intimately casual dining room, but the atmosphere, prices and array of cheeses, cold meats, Middle Eastern-influenced snacks, hearty soups and salads all hit the right spot. Try the pâté selection or the vegetable plate with melted goat's cheese. It gets packed, so be prepared to queue as bookings aren't taken. Open late.

Enoteca al Parlamento Achilli

Via dei Prefetti 15; tel: 06-687 3446; www.enotecalparlamento.com; Mon–Sat 10am–midight; €€€

Located right in front of the Italian Parliament building, this small Michelin starred restaurant is a favourite among politicians and journalists. The menu is varied and seasonal and follows the main rules of Roman cuisine – with some imaginative detours. Discreet service and intimate atmosphere, and, of course, fabulous wines.

Lost Food Factory

Via della Maddalena 50; tel: 392-655 5160; Sun–Mon 11am–8pm, Tue–Thu 11am–9pm, Fri–Sat 11am–9.30pm; €

Close to the Pantheon, this is the perfect place for a quick meal to refuel. Cheap prices, delicious paninis, and an extensive menu. Vegetarian and vegan options are available.

Maccheroni

Piazza delle Coppelle 44; tel: 06-6830 7895; www.ristorantemaccheroni.com; daily 12.30–3pm, 7–11pm; €€

Simple pasta dishes, seasonal greens, roast lamb and excellent desserts are served in a former butcher's shop. Always a popular spot in the city centre.

Obicà

Via dei Prefetti 26a (on Piazza di Firenze); tel: 06-683 2630; www.obica.com; Mon–Fri 8am– midnight, Sat–Sun 9am–midnight; €€€€

Obicà means 'here it is!' in the Neapolitan dialect, and this place has it. A foodie heaven, Obica is modern with a menu dedicated to multiple types of fresh mozzarella. They offer side dishes and great wines to accompany the cheese.

O' Pazzariello

Via Banco di Santo Spirito 19; tel: 06-6819 2641; daily noon–midnight; €

With an exhibitionist pizza-cook and pleasant waiters, this is a sure bet for a fun and affordable evening. The pizzas are thick-crusted and range from small to gigantic.

Osteria dell'Ingegno

Piazza di Pietra 45; tel: 06-678 0662; www. osteriadellingegno.com; daily noon–midnight; €€

Much frequented by politicians due to its location near parliament, this modern osteria specialises in light, inventive dishes. The sweets are homemade and the wines well chosen.

L'Osteria de Memmo

Via dei Soldati 22-23; tel: 06-6813 5277; www.osteriadememmo.it; Mon–Sat noon–11.30pm; €€€

In an old palazzo, three elegant rooms have been made over in modern minimalist style. The menu is creative, though first courses are a bit hit and miss. However, the main courses, desserts and wines compensate for any shortcomings.

La Rosetta

Via della Rosetta 8; tel: 06-686 1002; www. larosettaristorante.it; daily noon–11pm; €€€€

One of the best seafood restaurants in Rome, where the produce is guaranteed to have been caught that morning and prepared by an experienced chef. Unless you go for the 'working lunch' or a set-price degustazione (tasting) menu, your bill is likely to tip the €100-a-head mark for a full meal.

Terra di Siena

Piazza Pasquino 77–78; tel: 06-6830 7704; www.ristoranteterradisiena.com; daily noon–11.30pm; €€

Carnivores flock to this family-run restaurant, with dishes including succulent beef tagliata and the famed Fiorentina steak. The menu is 100 percent Tuscan, and portions are generous. The wine list includes a wide variety of Chianti labels.

Campo de' Fiori and the Ghetto

Baghetto Milky

Via del Portico d'Ottavia 2a; tel: 06-6830

0077; www.baghetto.com; Sun–Thu 11am–11pm, Fri 11am–3pm, Sat 7–11.30pm; €€

This certified kosher restaurant serves a meatless combination of Jewish-Roman and Middle Eastern specialities including Jewish-style artichokes, spicy fish (*hraimi*), and many Roman-Jewish vegetable dishes.

Cantina Lucifero

Via del Pellegrino 53; tel: 06 8976 7575; Tue–Sun 6pm–midnight; €€

This family-run eatery looks more like a wine bar than a proper restaurant, but serves delicious hot dishes nevertheless. In addition to lots of cheeses and cured meats, they make perfectly cooked steaks, tartars, cheese fondue, and many pasta specials.

Dar Filettaro a Santa Barbara

Largo dei Librari 88; tel: 06-686 4018; Mon–Sat 5.30–11pm; €

This is the Roman version of a fish and chip shop. Golden pieces of battered and fried salt cod are wrapped in paper and served with sautéed courgettes and beer. There is outdoor seating on the piazza in summer.

Osteria Romana di Simmi

Via di San Paolo alla Regola 29-31; tel: 06-686 1917; www.osteriaromana.it; Mon–Sat 12–3pm, 7–11pm; €€€€

This is a charming place located on a side piazza. Mountains of vegetables and appetisers greet your arrival. The understated elegance has been a favourite of visiting dignitaries.

Piperno

Via Monte de'Cenci 9; tel: 06-6860 6629; www.ristorantepiperno.it; Tue–Sun 12.45–2.15pm, Tue–Sat 7.45–10.15pm; €€€

One of the oldest restaurants in the Ghetto, up and running since 1860. This lovely trattoria serves many typical Roman Jewish kosher-style dishes, such as fried artichoke and sweetbreads, and baked fish.

Via Veneto and Villa Borghese

Il Fellini

Via Sicilia 150; tel: 327 194 6951; www.ilfellini.com; daily 6.30–11.30pm; €€€

The modern yet rustic interior creates a romantic ambiance. Catch of the day is served, simply cooked with similarly fresh sides; the pistachio crusted tuna fillet with baby spinach salad is a favourite. Excellent service.

Caffè Ciampini

Piazza Trinitá dei Monti 2; tel: 06-678 5678; www.caffeciampini.com; daily 8am–midnight, open from Mar to Nov only; €€

This restaurant provides a great place to relax with views, cool breezes and atmosphere. It is an affordable choice on the Pincio. Perfect for before or after a day at the Villa Borghese. Their signature dish is 'Tartufo al cioccolato'.

Ristorante Sardegna

Via Sardegna 34/36; tel: 06-4201 6296;

Pasta of all shapes and sizes

www.ristorantesardegna.it; daily noon–3pm, 7–11pm; €€€€

This high-end Sardinian restaurant serves fresh fish and seafood, with both cooked and raw options. Try the delicious pasta with fish roe and *seadas* and the traditional dessert consisting of a large *raviolo* filled with pecorino cheese and topped with honey.

La Terrazza at Eden

Via Ludovisi 49; tel: 06-4781 2752; www. dorchestercollection.com/en/rome/hotel-eden/restaurants-bars/la-terrazza; Wed–Mon 7–11.30pm; closed three weeks in Jan; €€€€

La Terrazza in the Hotel Eden is considered the most romantic view in Rome. The hushed environment, perfect service and succulent dishes add up to an unforgettable, if expensive, meal. Jacket and tie, and reservations, are essential.

Trastevere and the Gianicolo

Antica Pesa

Via Garibaldi 18; tel: 06-580 9236; www. anticapesa.it; Mon–Sat 7.30–11pm; €€€

Antica Pesa serves elegant Roman dishes such as ravioli with a white truffle sauce as well as seasonal chef's specialities. The wine list is very good, and the patio garden is perfect for relaxing and celebrity-spotting.

Bir and Fud

Via Benedetta 23; tel: 06-589 4016; http:// birandfud.it; Mon, Thu–Sun noon–late, Tue–Wed 6pm–late; €€€

This modern-day beer house specializes on small breweries from both Italy and abroad, and has a long craft beer menu to accompany the great food. The pizzas are some of the best in the city, and each dish is the result of extensive ingredient research and of a series of creative experiments that always turn out successful.

Checco er Carettiere

Via Benedetta 10; tel: 06-581 7018; www. checcoercarettiere.it; daily 12.30–3pm, 7.30pm–midnight; €€

A beloved and well-worn trattoria with a classic Trastevere feel. This popular place is always packed, and the menu caters to the hearty Roman worker with the classics. Homely, filling and really authentic. They have a surprisingly decent selection of local wines.

Meridionale

Via dei Fienaroli 30a; tel: 06-589 7196; www. meridionaletrastevere.com; daily 7–11pm; €€

A popular spot for both atmosphere and food. The walls are colourful and the design young and welcoming, and the cuisine is 100 percent southern Italian with a creative touch.

Roma Sparita

Piazza Santa Cecilia 24; tel: 06-580 0757; www.romasparita.com; Tue–Sun 12.30–2.30pm, 7–11pm; €€

A good choice for a lazy lunch after wandering the streets of Trastevere. Both the price and location have made this osteria popular for generations. Their menu

has all of the Roman classics, and they serve the *cacio e pepe* in a basket made of toasted parmesan.

Aventino and Testaccio

Da Oio a Casa Mia

Via Galvani 43; tel: 06-578 2680; Mon–Sat 12.30–11.30pm; €€

An unpretentious family-run trattoria with bags of atmosphere. Serves up classic pasta dishes in rich meaty sauces. If you like offal, try the *rigatoni alla pajata* (lamb's intestines).

Perilli

Via Marmorata 39; tel: 06-575 5100; Thu–Tue 12.30–3pm, 7.30–11.30pm; €€€

Perilli has been in business for nearly 100 years, happily serving long relaxed dinners in Roman style. The outdated interior and bow-tied waiters add charm and nostalgia. Pastas are tossed tableside, and they specialize in meat cut and cooked in a hundred ways (it was once a stone's throw from the main slaughterhouse and butchers).

Celio, Monti and Esquilino

Osteria La Sol Fa

Via Germano Sommeiller 19; tel: 06-702 7996; www.osterialasolfa.it; Mon–Fri 12.30–2.30pm and 7.30–10.30pm, Sat evening only; €€

This family-run restaurant features a select menu of fresh pastas, veal, oxtail and meat and fish of the day options, all served in a classic Italian setting. This is homemade Roman cuisine at its finest.

La Carbonara

Via Panisperna 214; tel: 06-482 5176; www. lacarbonara.it; Mon–Sat 12.30–2.30pm, 7–11pm; €€

This excellent trattoria is just out of the way enough to have great food and local atmosphere. The signature dish is, of course, *pasta alla carbonara*; their grilled meats are good too.

La Cicala e la Formica

Via Leonina 17; tel: 06-481 7490; http:// lacicalaelaformica.it; daily 12.30–11pm; €€

In the heart of Monti is this tiny little trattoria with a handful of tables on the street. They serve freshly made pastas and a number of seasonal dishes. The vegetables and fish are from the local market. The kitchen is closed from 3–6.30pm however, you can still stop in for a drink.

Hostaria I Clementini

Via San Giovanni in Laterano 106; tel: 06-4542 6395; daily noon–5pm, 7–10pm; €

This is a little osteria located in the heart of the Celio across from San Clemente. It serves up simple but consistently good fare. Try the pasta with mussels or the fried appetizer.

La Gallina Bianca

Via Rosmini 5–12; tel: 06-4743 777; www. lagallinabiancaroma.it; daily noon–midnight; €€

There are not a lot of dishes on the menu, but each dish is prepared with great care at this excellent trattoria. Ingredients are hand picked by the chef and cooked to perfection.

Performance at Casa del Jazz

NIGHTLIFE

From historic theatres to state-of-the-art concert venues and intimate jazz clubs to dance hotspots, Rome has something for every night owl. In the city's clubs, things typically get going late, but once midnight strikes, the hordes pour in, and the night gives over to the beats of house, hip-hop and electronic – Rome's favourite dance-club soundtracks.

Theatre

English Theatre of Rome

Teatro Arciliuto, Piazza di Montevecchio, 5; tel: 06-687 9419; www.rometheatre.com; bus: 30, 70, 81, 87
This small but centrally located venue has an October–June season with innovative productions in English.

Teatro Argentina

Largo Argentina 52; tel: 06-6840 00311; www.teatrodiroma.net; bus: 30, 40, 46, 62, 64, 70, 81, 87, 492; tram: 8
Rome's premier theatre has a plush 1730s interior and stages an extensive repertoire of quality classic and contemporary productions as well also putting on dance shows.

Teatro Ghione

Via delle Fornaci 37; tel: 06-637 2294; www.teatroghione.it; bus: 64
An intimate theatre with its own company. Productions are focused on Italian classics and comedy.

Teatro India

Lungotevere Vittorio Gassman 1; tel: 06-8775 2210; www.teatrodiroma.net; bus: 170, 766, 775
This avant-garde theatre is located near the old power plant in Testaccio and has several performance spaces. Productions are often first runs.

Teatro Mongiovino

Via Giovanni Genocchi 15; tel: 06 513 9405; www.accettellateatro.it; bus: 160, 669, 671, 716
This theatre specialises in acts for children and young people with puppet performances and shows conducted in a colourful garden space.

Music

Auditorium Parco della Musica

Viale Pietro de Coubertin 30; tel: 06-802411; www.auditorium.com; bus: 53, 168, 910, 982, tram 2
Architect Renzo Piano's Auditorium complex is one of the city's newest buildings. More than five performance spaces have been created to stage a wide variety of superb classical, jazz and rock concerts and shows.

Casa del Jazz

Viale di Porta Ardeatina 55; tel: 06-8024 1281; www.casajazz.it; bus: 30, 77, 671, 714
This lovely villa by the Aurelian walls – a former crime headquarters – was

Auditorium Parco Della Musica

confiscated by the city and turned into the 'house of jazz'. The rich programme includes Italian and international jazz stars. The large garden makes for pleasant evenings under the stars.

Gregory's
Via Gregoriana 54; tel: 06-679 6386; www.gregorysjazz.com; metro: Barberini
This intimate, retro club has an excellent line-up of traditional jazz as well as experimental jam sessions. Closed Mon.

Teatro dell'Opera
Piazza Beniamino Gigli 1; tel: 06-481 7003; www.operaroma.it; metro: Repubblica
Rome's opera house, also the home of the national ballet, was constructed in 1879 to compete with Milan's La Scala; the acoustics are nearly perfect. Productions range from Peter Greenaway to Puccini to Debussy.

Teatro Palladium
Piazza Bartolomeo Romano 8; tel: 06-5733 2772; www.teatropalladium.uniroma3.it; bus: 670, metro: Garbatella
The programme at this multi-functional performance space includes international music as well as performance art, spoken word and modern dance.

Villa Ada
Via di Ponte Salario; www.villaada.org; bus: 63, 83, 310, 92
Music events, concerts and summer festivals are hosted in this large park.

Planet Rome
Via del Commercio 36; tel: 06-574 7826; www.planetroma.it; metro: Ostiense
This large multi-level club has three dance floors. Guest DJs and live acts.

Ice Club
Via della Madonna dei Monti; tel: 06-9784 5581; http://iceclubroma.it; Metro: Cavour
Beat the sweltering summer heat in this kitschy ice bar. The cover charge to enter includes a vodka drink.

Circolo Degli Illuminati
Via Giuseppe Libetta 1; tel: 327 761 5286; https://circolodegliilluminati.it; Metro: Garbatella
With three different rooms and a garden space this venue offers a wide variety of music. Famous for their Saturday night Minù.

Goa
Via Libetta 13; tel: 06-574 8277; www.goaclub.com; bus: 23, 769, 792, N2; metro: Garbatella
The temple of electronic music in Rome, with the best DJs. Packed on Saturdays.

Shilling
Piazzale Cristoforo Colombo 25; tel: 06-5647 0728; www.shillingclub.it; metro: Cristoforo Colombo (overground)
Designed like a tropical island, with a bar, restaurant and beachfront dance spaces, this place is one of Ostia's best night hotspots. Great music.

A–Z

A

Admission fees

Museum admission fees vary greatly, but the major ones range from €7–16. Most state or municipal museums offer free entrance to citizens under 18 or over 65. The entrance ticket to the Roman Forum can be used to visit the Colosseum and the Palatine Hill. Entrance to the Pantheon and all basilicas and churches is free, as is entrance to the Vatican Museums on the last Sunday of the month (expect long queues).

B

Business hours

In general shops open Mon–Sat 9am–1 or 1.30pm and 3.30–7.30pm. Many shops and restaurants close for two weeks in August. Churches typically open 7am–7pm with a three-hour lunch break (times vary). Banks open roughly Mon–Fri between 8.30am–5 or 6pm; a few in the city centre also open on Saturday morning. Many state and city museums are closed on Mondays.

Bike rental

Using a bicycle is a great way to get around the city centre or to visit the green areas of Villa Borghese and the Appia Antica. Bike rentals charge around €4 per hour and between €12 and €15 for the whole day. Bici & Baci (www.bici-baci.com) has four rental spots at Via del Viminale 5, Via Cavour 302, Via Rosmini 25, and Vicolo del Bottino 8, while Collalti (www.collaltibici.com) is a reliable shop on Via del Pellegrino 82. Riding a bike can be challenging in traffic, so stick to the pedestrian areas of the city centre, bike-friendly Prati, and the bike lane along the Tiber.

C

Children

Little ones are welcome everywhere. Villa Borghese park (see page 58) offers plenty of outdoor entertainment, with paddleboats, bike rentals and expansive green space. The Bioparco (zoo) is located on the grounds, and there's also a playhouse, a kids' movie theatre and a puppet theatre in the Pincio Gardens. Nearby, the Explora Children's Museum (see page 23) is packed with interactive exhibits and kid-sized dioramas, all aimed to teach and entertain.

Clothing

Light summer clothes are suitable from spring to autumn. The Roman heat is sometimes alleviated by a sea breeze during the day and evenings can be cool, even in summer, so keep a jacket

on hand. Hats and sunglasses are recommended for sun protection.

Rainfall is rare in mid-summer, but when the deluge does come, it's often a surprise afternoon shower that rarely lasts for long. November to January is notoriously rainy, so bring your raincoat. In winter, you'll want to dress in layers. For climate information, see page 14.

Crime

The main problem tourists experience in Rome is petty crime: pick-pocketing and bag snatching, together with theft from parked cars. Leave money and valuables in a safe place, and keep an eye on your wallet. Be especially vigilant on crowded buses.

Report a theft *(furto)* to the police as soon as possible: you will need the police report for any insurance claim and to replace stolen documents. For information on the nearest police station call the Questura Centrale, 15 Via San Vitale, tel: 06-468 61 or ask for the *questura più vicina*.

Customs

Visitors from EU countries are not obliged to declare goods imported into or exported from Italy if they are for personal use, up to the following limits: 800 cigarettes, 200 cigars or 1kg of tobacco; 10 litres of spirits (over 22 percent alcohol) or 20 litres of fortified wine (under 22 percent alcohol).

For US citizens, the duty-free allowance is 200 cigarettes, 50 cigars or 250g tobacco; 1 litre of spirits or 2 litres of wine; one 100ml bottle of perfume and duty-free gifts to the value of US$200–800 depending on how often you travel.

Disabled travellers

Rome is a difficult city for people with disabilities. However, things are improving, and the following have installed ramps and lifts: the Vatican Museums, Galleria Doria Pamphilj, Castel Sant'Angelo, Palazzo Venezia, the Vittorio Emanuele monument, St Peter's, Galleria Borghese and the Colosseum.

For information on disabled access, contact Roma Per Tutti (tel: 06-5717 7094, www.romapertutti.it).

E

Electricity

Standard is 220 volts AC, 50 cycles. Sockets have either two or three round pins. For UK visitors, adaptors can be bought before you leave home, or at airports and stations. Travellers from the US will need a transformer.

Embassies and consulates

If your passport is lost or stolen you will need to obtain a police report *(see Crime)* and have proof of your identity to get a new one.

Australia: 5 Via Antonio Bosio; tel: 06-852 721; www.italy.embassy.gov.au

Italian policemen

Canada: Consulate office, 30 Via Zara; tel: 06-854 441; www.canadainternational.gc.ca

Ireland: Villa Spada, Via Giacomo Medici; tel: 06-585 2381; www.ambasciata-irlanda.it

New Zealand: 44 Via Clitunno; tel: 06-853 7501; www.mfat.govt.nz

South Africa: 14 Via Tanaro; tel: 06-852 541; http://lnx.sudafrica.it

UK: 80a Via XX Settembre; tel: 06-4220 0001; http://ukinitaly.fco.gov.uk

US: 121 Via Veneto; tel: 06-46741; https://it.usembassy.gov

Emergency numbers

Police 113, Carabinieri 112, Fire 115, Ambulance 118.

Health

EU residents are entitled to the same medical treatment as an Italian citizen. Visitors will need to obtain an EHIC card (www.ehic.org.uk) before they go.

US citizens are advised to take out private health insurance. Canadian and Australian citizens are covered by a reciprocal arrangements between their governments and the Italian governments. Call your local health office before leaving to confirm what is covered.

Chemists. These *(farmacie)* can easily be identified by their sign with a green cross on it. Farmacia della Stazione, 51 Piazza dei Cinquecento (corner of Via Cavour), tel: 06-488 0019, and Farmacia Piram Omeopatia, 228 Via Nazionale, tel: 06-488 4437, with the latter open 24 hours.

Emergencies. If you need emergency treatment, call 118 for an ambulance or to get information on the nearest hospital with an emergency department *(pronto soccorso)*.

Hospitals. The most central hospital is Ospedale Fatebenefratelli, Isola Tiberina, tel: 06-68371. If your child is sick, Ospedale Pediatrico Bambino Gesù (4 Piazza Sant'Onofrio, tel: 06-68591) is a highly regarded paediatric hospital.

Internet

Many of the city's green spaces are now wireless hotspots; you can surf the internet free in villas Borghese, Pamphilj, Ada and Torlonia. RomaWireless provides Wi-Fi coverage to public places through 1300 hotspots across the city. They offer 4 hours free Internet per day, but you must have an Italian sim card to complete the registration process. If you are traveling without your laptop, you can use one of the computers in one of the many call centres/internet cafés around Termini station and Piazza Vittorio Emanuele.

Useful websites

Information on cultural events: www.turismoroma.it

Vatican Museums: www.vatican.va

Souvenirs by the Colosseum

Rome City Council: www.comune.roma.it
Roman museums: www.museiincomune.it
Hotel Reservations: tourist offices, 06-0608
Rome airports: www.adr.it

L

Language

You will not find English spoken everywhere in Rome, as you do in some other European cities. However, Italians are usually helpful and quick to understand what you want. Italians appreciate foreigners making an effort to speak their language, even if it's only a few words. In the major hotels and shops, staff usually speak some English. For useful vocabulary, see page 134.

Left luggage

You can leave your luggage at Termini Station with KiPoint for a per hour, per bag fee. Fiumicino Airport also has 24-hour left-luggage facilities in the international terminals.

LGBTQ travellers

Slowly, but surely, the capital is inching its way toward becoming a more tolerant and gay-friendly city. A number of bars, restaurants and clubs have opened up within the city centre, and welcome a mixed crowd.

Arcigay Roma, Via Zabaglia 14; tel: 06-6450 1102 (Mon–Sat 4–8pm); www.arcigayroma.it; metro and bus: Piramide. This branch of the Italian Arcigay association serves as a meeting and information point, and a centre for social activism. Many clubs require an Arcigay membership card, which can be purchased on site.

Circolo Mario Mieli di Cultura Omosessuale, 2A Via Efeso; tel: 06-541 3985; www.mariomieli.org; Mon–Fri 11am–6pm; metro: San Paolo, bus: 23. Rome's most respected gay, lesbian and transgender organisation serves as a cultural and counselling centre; its website is a viable resource for all things gay in the city.

Rainbow Line, tel: 800-110 611; hotline for those seeking help or advice related to gay issues.

Lost property

For property lost on trains anywhere in Rome ask at the Termini Station's left-luggage office, located at the underground level (-1) near platform 24, open from 6am–midnight.

For property lost on public transport (except trains) contact the bus and tram network (ATAC) lost property office: tel: 06-6769 3214; www.atac.roma.it; Mon, Tue, Wed and Fri 8.30am–1pm; Thu 8.30am–5pm.

M

Maps

Free city maps are available from the tourist offices (see page 130). Trans-

Tables on Piazza Navone

port maps can be downloaded from the ATAC website (www.atac.roma.it), while more detailed transport maps (called Roma MetroBus) can be bought at any newsstand in the centre.

Media

Most important European dailies are available on the day of publication from street kiosks in the city centre, as is the *New York Times International Edition*.

The main Rome-based Italian newspapers are *La Repubblica* and *Il Messaggero*. Other Italian newspapers such as *Il Corriere della Sera* offer Rome editions with local news and entertainment listings.

The free monthly magazine WHERE ROME (www.whererome.com), available from hotel receptions, has a reliable editorial section that includes concert and exhibition calendars and a number of recommendations. *Wanted in Rome* (www.wantedinrome.com), a fortnightly magazine in English, is another good source of listings information. *The American Magazine* (www.theamericanmag.com) is a monthly magazine on Italian cultural life.

Money

The unit of currency in Italy is the euro (€), which is divided into 100 cents. There are 5, 10, 20, 50, 100, 200 and 500 euro notes, coins that are worth €1 and €2, and 1, 2, 5, 10, 20 and 50 cent coins.

Changing money. You need your passport or identification card when changing money, which can be a slow operation. Not all banks will provide cash against a credit card, and some may refuse to cash travellers' cheques in certain currencies. On the whole, the larger banks (those with a national or international network) will be the best for tourist transactions. Travellers' cheques are generally the safest way to carry money around, but they are much less prevalent now and banks charge a large commission for cashing them.

Credit and debit cards. While major credit cards are accepted by most hotels, shops and restaurants, it is best to keep some cash on hand, as the card-reading machines are frequently out of order.

Cash machines (ATMs), called *bancomat*, can be found throughout central Rome, and are the easiest and generally the cheapest way of obtaining cash.

Tipping. Service is not included in a restaurant bill unless noted on the menu as *servizio*. It is customary to leave a modest tip, but nothing like the 10 to 15 percent common in other countries. Romans usually leave between €1–5, but tourists are expected to be slightly more generous. When you take a taxi, just round the fare up to the nearest euro.

P

Post

Post offices are generally open Mon–Fri 8.30am–1pm; central post offices are generally open in the afternoon, too.

Post box   Roman newspaper

Stamps (francobolli) can be bought at many tobacconists (tabacchi). Italian postboxes are red or yellow, but blue boxes specifically for foreign letters have been set up in the centre. Postboxes have two slots, per la città (for Rome) and tutte le altre destinazioni (everywhere else).

For delivery to Europe (up to three days) and to the rest of the world (up to five days), ask for posta prioritaria (priority post) stamps.

The main post office is in Piazza San Silvestro, off Via del Corso (Mon–Fri 8am–7pm, Sat until 12.35pm). The post office at Termini train station is open Mon–Fri (8am–7pm) and until 12.35pm on Sat.

Public holidays

1 Jan New Year's Day
6 Jan Epiphany
Easter Monday
25 Apr Liberation Day
1 May Labour Day
2 June Founding of the Republic
29 June Sts Peter and Paul Day (Rome only)
15 Aug The Assumption of Mary
1 Nov All Saints' Day
8 Dec Immaculate Conception
25–26 Dec Christmas and St Stephen's Day

Holidays and festivals

New Year's Eve is very big business in Rome: drinking, dancing, noisy midnight celebrations with firecrackers. It falls in the middle of a long holiday period that starts on Christmas Eve and lasts until Epiphany on 6 January. Starting 1 December, there is an annual Christmas Market in Piazza Navona.

Easter is normally a three- or four-day religious holiday, though businesses only close on Easter Sunday and Monday. On Good Friday there is a procession from the Palatine to the Colosseum (Via Crucis), during which the Pope or a high-level cardinal walks the Stations of the Cross. On Easter Sunday, many people head for St Peter's Square at noon for the Pope's traditional Urbi et Orbi blessing. The saints' days of St Joseph (19 March) and St John (24 June) are celebrated with special dishes.

The city empties in August when many Romans go on holiday (especially around the Feast of the Assumption on 15 August, referred to as Ferragosto). However, in recent years, the city council has put on an incredible range of outdoor concerts and other cultural events from June to September, and the city is less deserted than it used to be.

T

Telephones

The very few payphones left (located mainly at the airport) accept credit cards, but fares can be high. There are a number of inexpensive international phone cards available from newsstands, and there are also call centres

Segway tour

(especially near Termini station) where you can make your call and pay later.

For a number outside Italy, first dial 00 (the international access code), then the country code, the area code (omitting the initial 0, if applicable) and then the subscriber number.

Calling Rome. Landlines in Rome have an 06 area code which you must use whether calling from within Rome, from outside Rome or from abroad. Most numbers in Rome have four to eight digits. Toll-free numbers start with 800.

Mobile phone numbers begin with 3, for example 338, 340, 333 or 348, and cost a lot more.

Time zones

Italy follows Central European Time (GMT+1). From the last Sunday in March to the last Sunday in September, clocks are advanced one hour (GMT+2).

Toilets

Bars should let you use their toilets, though this does not always happen. Many of the small bars in the centre will just tell you the toilet is out of service. When the toilet does work, bar owners may throw you a look if you don't spend any money at the bar first. In many cases, bar toilets are locked and you will need to ask for the key (*chiave*) at the till; once inside you may find out that there is no soap or toilet paper. There are however a few public pay toilets near most of the major sights and monuments.

Tourist information

The following **tourist information points** or PIT (*punto informativo turistico*) are open daily 9.30am–7pm:

Piazza Pia (Castel Sant'Angelo); Via dei Fori Imperiali; Piazza delle Cinque Lune (Piazza Navona); Via Nazionale (Palazzo delle Esposizioni); Via Giolitti (Termini); Via Marco Minghetti (Trevi Fountain).

The city council offers a tourism information line (tel: 060608; www.060608.it) with information in English available from 9am–7pm.

The PIT Tourist Offices or its multilingual call centre 060608 (daily 9am–7pm) will make commission-free reservations for you. There is also an information point in Termini Station. It opens daily 8am–6.45pm.

The **Vatican Tourist Office** (Ufficio Pellegrini e Turisti) is in Braccio Carlo Magno, Piazza San Pietro (to the left of the basilica), tel: 06-6988 2350 (Mon–Sat 9am–6.30pm).

Tourist information abroad

Italian Government Tourist Office: 686 Park Ave, New York 10111; tel: 212-245 5618.

Italian National Tourist Board - Australia & New Zealand: 40 William St, East Sydney NSW 2011; tel: +61 2 9357 2561.

Tours

If you want a tour tailored to your needs, Rome is the city to find it. But be aware

that Italy has strict regulations on licensing for tour guides. Many of the tour hawkers in the Forum and Vatican areas are working illegally.

For classic group bus tours, check out Carrani Tours (Via Ignazio Pettinengo 72; tel: 06-432 181; www.carrani.com) and Green Line Tours (Via Giovanni Amendola 32; tel: 06-482 7480; www.greenlinetours.com).

For the intellectual traveller, Context Travel (tel: 015 897 7508; www.context-travel.com/cities/rome) offers small group and private walking tours lead by art historians and archaeologists.

Transport

Arrival by air

Travellers on scheduled flights land at the main airport, Aeroporto Leonardo da Vinci (tel: 06-65951) in Fiumicino, about 30km (18 miles) southwest of Rome. Some flights arrive at Ciampino airport (tel: 06-65951), about 15km (9 miles) to the southeast. For more information, see www.adr.it.

Airport transport. From Fiumicino airport, trains run to Termini Station every 30 minutes from 6.38am until 11.38pm. There is also an infrequent late-night bus service. If you take a taxi, choose only a white one with a meter. Be prepared to pay a fixed taxi fare of €48 from/to Fiumicino to/from inside the Aurelian Walls (includes 4 passengers, luggage and all extra fees). The fixed fare from Ciampino to the city centre is €30. Beware of fraudulent taxi

drivers and report any problems by calling 06-06 08; a COTRAL bus runs twice hourly to the Anagnina metro station.

A private bus service runs frequently between Ciampino airport and the city in conjunction with Ryanair and easy-Jet flights (www.terravision.it). For a limousine service, for airport pick-up and tours of Rome, contact Airport Connection Services (tel: 338-987 6465; www.airportconnection.it).

Arrival by rail

If you are travelling from other parts of Italy or Europe, most trains arrive at the main Roman station, Termini. Like bus and metro tickets, train tickets must be validated at a yellow machine in the station before boarding. For routes, ticketing and reservations, see www.trenitalia.it or www.italotreno.it.

Arrival by bus

If you are travelling by bus both on national or international services, you are likely to arrive on Via Marsala near Termini or the bus terminal at Tiburtina Station.

Arrival by car

Car travellers arriving in Rome from any direction first hit the Grande Raccordo Anulare (GRA), the ring motorway. The A1 (Autostrada del Sole) leads into the GRA from both north and south, as does the A24 from the east. If you arrive on the Via del Mare from the coast (Ostia), you can either join the GRA or continue straight into the city centre.

Roman taxis are white

The various roads into the centre lead off the GRA. For the north, choose the exits Via Salaria, Via Flaminia or Via Nomentana. If heading for the Vatican area, follow the GRA to the west and take the exit Via Aurelia. If you're going south, take the Via Tuscolana, Via Appia Nuova, Via Pontina (which leads into the Via Cristoforo Colombo) or the Via del Mare.

When leaving the GRA, follow the white signs to the road you want rather than the blue ones, which usually lead away from the centre. The city-centre sign is a black dot in the middle of a black circle on a white background.

Transport within Rome

Taxis. Meters in white taxis tend to start at around €3. After 10pm, on Sundays and for luggage there is a surcharge. You can order a radio taxi by phone (tel: 06-3570), which start their meters upon your acceptance (the automated operator will give you an approximate wait time and prompt you to hang up the phone to accept). Fares are some of the highest in Europe, so be prepared to pay.

Buses and trams. Tobacco stores displaying a big 'T' sell metro-tram-bus tickets, without which you are not supposed to board a bus. Tickets are available as: a single ride €1.50, all-day pass €7, 3-day pass €18 and weekly €24.

Once on board, stamp your ticket in the machine on board. There's a fine if you're caught without a ticket or without having stamped it. City bus services are operated by ATAC (www.atac.roma.it).

There are a large number of bus tours offered throughout the city including the hop-on, hop-off tour. Check at either Termini Station or at the Vatican for options.

Metro. The metro is a skeletal system with only three lines. A and B intersect at Termini. The "C" line opened in 2014 but is being developed further. It connects to the rest of the system at San Giovanni (A). The Metro operates daily 5.30am–11.30pm (until 1.30am Friday–Saturday). A shuttle bus service (MA1 and MA2) substitutes the stops when there's a problem on the line, but calculate time for traffic. From Piramide, there's a train to Ostia (Ostia Antica and beaches), a stop on the metro line B, and the 23 bus to Trastevere and the Vatican.

Construction and closures takes place randomly and often so check before you travel.

For more information and a handy route planner, visit www.atac.roma.it.

Trains. Should you want to leave the city by train, you might find Termini Station a frustrating experience with long queues at the enquiries and ticket desks in summer. You are likely to get better service from the city's travel agencies. Tickets must be stamped before boarding at one of the yellow machines in the station.

For information call 892021 or see www.trenitalia.com. Tickets can be

Rome's metro is minimal

bought online or by phone, and picked up (or bought directly) from one of the self-service machines at the station. The other major rail company, Italo (www.italotreno.it) operates high-speed trains between Milan and Naples and offers discounted tickets if you book well ahead.

Driving. Driving a car through Rome's tangled streets can be an exercise in frustration. Rental cars are available from the airport or Termini station from the following:

Avis (tel: 06-481 4373; www.avis.com); Europcar (tel: 06 7934 0387; www. europcar.com); Hertz (tel: 06 488 3967; www.hertz.it); Maggiore (tel: 06 488 0049; www.maggiore.it); Sixt (tel: 02-9475 7979; www.sixt.it).

Most car-rental agencies have pick-up points around the city. Look out for the electronic screens with cameras indicating the restricted traffic areas (ZTL) around the historic centre. *Varco attivo* means traffic is currently restricted (do not enter); *varco non attivo* means you can go. The centre is usually closed to cars between 7am and 6pm, but times may vary.

Petrol. Petrol stations *(benzinaio)* are scattered across the city and generally follow business hours. Rates vacillate around €1.50 a litre. For unleaded ask for *senza piombo*. Many stations accept credit cards and all accept cash. Outside the city, you may need cash.

Visas

EU passport-holders do not require a visa, just a valid passport or ID card. Visitors from the US, Canada, Australia and New Zealand do not require visas for stays of up to three months; non-EU citizens need a full passport.

Nationals of most other countries do need a visa. This must be obtained in advance from the nearest Italian Embassy.

A traditional tram

Italian door sign

LANGUAGE

Italian is relatively easy to pick up, if you have any knowledge of French or Spanish (or a grounding in Latin). Most hotels have staff who speak some English, and unless you go well off the beaten track, you should have little problem communicating in shops or restaurants. However, there are places not on the tourist circuit where you will have the chance to practise your Italian, and local people will think more of you for making an effort. Here are a few basics to help you get started.

Useful phrases

General
Yes *Sì*
No *No*
Thank you *Grazie*
Many thanks *Mille grazie/Tante grazie*
You're welcome *Prego*
All right/That's fine *Va bene*
Please *Per favore/Per cortesia*
Excuse me (to get attention) *Scusi*
Excuse me (in a crowd) *Permesso*
Could you help me? (formal) *Potrebbe aiutarmi?*
Certainly *Ma, certo/Certamente*
Can you show me...? *Può indicarmi...?*
Can you help me, please? *Può aiutarmi, per cortesia?*
I need... *Ho bisogno di...*
I'm lost *Mi sono perso*
I'm sorry *Mi dispiace*
I don't know *Non lo so*

I don't understand *Non capisco*
Do you speak English/French/Spanish? *Parla inglese/francese/spagnolo?*
Could you speak more slowly? *Può parlare più lentamente, per favore?*
Could you repeat that please? *Può ripetere, per piacere?*
How much does it cost? *quanto costa?*
this one/that one *questo/quello*
Have you got...? *Avete...?*

At a bar/restaurant
I'd like to book a table *Vorrei prenotare un tavolo*
Have you got a table for... *Avete un tavolo per...*
I have a reservation *Ho prenotato*
lunch *il pranzo*
supper *la cena*
I'm a vegetarian *Sono vegetariano/a*
May we have the menu? *Ci dia la carta?*
What would you like? *Che cosa prende?*
I'd like... *Vorrei...*
mineral water *acqua minerale*
fizzy/still *gasata/naturale*
a bottle of *una bottiglia di*
a glass of *un bicchiere di*
red wine *vino rosso*
white wine *vino bianco*
beer *una birra*

Numbers
One *uno*
Two *due*

Good words to know

One of Rome's best addresses

Three *tre*
Four *quattro*
Five *cinque*
Six *sei*
Seven *sette*
Eight *otto*
Nine *nove*
Ten *dieci*
Twenty *venti*
Thirty *trenta*
Forty *quaranta*
Fifty *cinquanta*
One hundred *cento*
One thousand *mille*

Getting around
What time do you open/close? *A che ora apre/chiude?*
Closed for the holidays *Chiuso per ferie*
Where can I buy tickets? *Dove posso fare i biglietti?*
What time does the train leave? *A che ora parte il treno?*
Can you tell me where to get off? *Mi può dire dove devo scendere?*
Where is the nearest bank/hotel? *Dov'è la banca/l'albergo più vicino?*
On the right *a destra*
On the left *a sinistra*
Go straight on *Va sempre diritto*

Online
Where's an internet cafe? *Dov'è un Internet caffè?*
Does it have wireless internet? *C'è il wireless?*
What is the Wi-Fi password? *Qual è la password Wi-Fi?*

Is the Wi-Fi free? *Il WiFi è gratis?*
How do I turn the computer on/off? *Come si accende/spegne il computer?*
Can I...? *Posso...?*
access the internet *collegarmi (a Internet)*
check e-mail *controllare le e-mail*
print *stampare*
plug in/charge my laptop/iPhone/ iPad? *collegare/ricaricare il mio portatile/iPhone/iPad?*
access Skype? *usare Skype?*
How much per hour/half hour? *Quanto costa per un'ora/mezz'ora?*
How do I...? *Come...?*
connect/disconnect *ci si collega/scollega*
log on/log off *si fa il login/logout*
What's your e-mail? *Qual è la sua e-mail?*
My e-mail is... *La mia e-mail è...*

Social media
Are you on Facebook/Twitter? *È su Facebook/Twitter? (polite form) Sei su Facebook/Twitter? (informal form)*
What's your user name? *Qual è il suo nome utente? (polite form) Qual è il tuo nome utente? (informal form)*
I'll add you as a friend. *La aggiungerò come amico. (polite form) Ti aggiungerò come amico. (informal form)*
I'll follow you on Twitter. *La seguirò su Twitter. (polite form) Ti seguirò su Twitter. (informal form)*
I'll put the pictures on Facebook/ Twitter. *Metterò le foto su Facebook/ Twitter.*

Anita Ekberg in 'La Dolce Vita'

BOOKS AND FILM

One of the most photogenic, evocative and romantic places in the world, and a highlight on the cultural circuit from ancient times through the Grand Tours of the 19th century, to the present day, Rome has been the inspiration for and the setting of a vast catalogue of literary works and films.

Rome's literary pedigree stretches back to the days of the Republic, when Cicero penned his hugely influential philosophical works and speeches, and the city has been inspiring dazzled writers ever since.

You can pay homage to literary luminaries at the residences of Keats, Shelley, Goethe and Alberto Moravia, head for the student quarter and hang out in a trendy book bar, or join the hordes of literature-hungry Romans at the city's Literature Festival in June.

As far as film goes, Rome was the birthplace of Italian cinema: the country's first feature, *La Presa di Roma* – a dramatic tale of unification – marked the beginning of the Eternal City's enduring love affair with celluloid.

Post-war Rome gave birth to Neo-Realism, an influential movement driven by some of the most acclaimed directors of their time, including Roberto Rossellini and Vittorio de Sica. Output was at the Cinecittà studios, a sort of Hollywood-on-the-Tiber founded by Mussolini and still in use (and indeed enjoying a resurgence) today.

Directors influenced by Neo-Realism included Pier Paolo Pasolini and Federico Fellini, who placed his adopted city under a microscope in *La Dolce Vita* (1960) and left us the enduring image of Anita Ekberg cooling off in the Trevi Fountain.

Today, Rome's most acclaimed filmmaker is Nanni Moretti, Italy's Woody Allen. The city is often centre stage in his films, notably where he scooters around the concrete suburbs in search of the essence of Rome. A star-studded international festival (www.romacinemafest.it) – a relative newcomer to the glamorous festival circuit – also promises to cement Rome's place on the cinematic map.

The list below includes our suggestions for the best background reading and cinematic viewing to get a greater feel for the Eternal City.

Books

History and society
The Early History of Rome, by Livy.
Daily Life in Ancient Rome, by Jérôme Carcopino.
The Roman Emperors, by Michael Grant.
The History of the Decline and Fall of the Roman Empire, by Edward Gibbon.

A History of Rome, by Michael Grant.
Rome: Biography of a City, by Christopher Hibbert.
The Italians, by Luigi Barzini.
The Dark Heart of Italy, by Tobias Jones.
Rubicon: the Last Years of the Roman Republic, by Tom Holland.

Art and literature
The Aeneid, by Virgil.
Meditations, by Marcus Aurelius.
Lives of the Artists, by Giorgio Vasari.
The Life of Benvenuto Cellini, by Benvenuto Cellini.
Rome, by Emile Zola.
Portrait of a Lady, by Henry James.
The Woman of Rome and Roman Tales, by Alberto Moravia.
A Violent Life, by Pier Paolo Pasolini.
I Claudius and **Claudius the God**, by Robert Graves.

Food and wine
Italian Food, by Elizabeth David.
The Essentials of Classic Italian Cooking, by Marcella Hazan.
Cooking the Roman Way, by David Downie

Famous travellers
Pictures from Italy, by Charles Dickens.
Italian Journey, by Johann Wolfgang von Goethe, translated by W.H. Auden & Elizabeth Mayer.
Italian Hours, by Henry James.
A Traveller in Rome, by Henry V. Morton.
Italy and the Grand Tour by Jeremy Black.
With Byron in Italy: A Selection of the Poems and Letters of Lord Byron Relating to His Life in Italy, by Anna Benneson McMahan.

'La Dolce Vita' poster

Film

Rome, Open City (Roma, città aperta; 1945)
Bicycle Thieves (Ladri di biciclette; 1948)
Quo Vadis (1951)
Roman Holiday (1953)
Ben-Hur (1959)
Cleopatra (1963)
La Dolce Vita (1960)
Dear Diary (Caro Diario; 1994)
Mid-August Lunch (Pranzo di Ferragosto; 2008)
To Rome with Love (2012)
The Great Beauty (2013)

ABOUT THIS BOOK

This *Explore Guide* has been produced by the editors of Insight Guides, whose books have set the standard for visual travel guides since 1970. With top-quality photography and authoritative recommendations, these guidebooks bring you the very best routes and itineraries in the world's most exciting destinations.

BEST ROUTES

The routes in the book provide something to suit all budgets, tastes and trip lengths. As well as covering the destination's many classic attractions, the itineraries track lesser-known sights, and there are also excursions for those who want to extend their visit outside the city. The routes embrace a range of interests, so whether you are an art fan, a gourmet, a history buff or have kids to entertain, you will find an option to suit.

We recommend reading the whole of a route before setting out. This should help you to familiarise yourself with it and enable you to plan where to stop for refreshments – options are shown in the 'Food and Drink' box at the end of each tour.

For our pick of the tours by theme, consult Recommended Routes for… (see pages 6–7).

INTRODUCTION

The routes are set in context by this introductory section, giving an overview of the destination to set the scene, plus background information on food and drink, shopping and more, while a succinct history timeline highlights the key events over the centuries.

DIRECTORY

Also supporting the routes is a Directory chapter, with a clearly organised A–Z of practical information, our pick of where to stay while you are there and select restaurant listings; these eateries complement the more low-key cafés and restaurants that feature within the routes and are intended to offer a wider choice for evening dining. Also included here are some nightlife listings, plus a handy language guide and our recommendations for books and films about the destination.

ABOUT THE AUTHORS

Solveig Steinhardt and Daniel Mosseri have spent years discovering the Eternal City's hidden treasures. Solveig regularly works as a correspondent for a number of travel magazines and guidebooks, and Daniel is a journalist and writer focusing on Italy's politics, history and cultural heritage.

CONTACT THE EDITORS

We hope you find this Explore Guide useful, interesting and a pleasure to read. If you have any questions or feedback on the text, pictures or maps, please do let us know. If you have noticed any errors or outdated facts, or have suggestions for places to include on the routes, we would be delighted to hear from you. Please drop us an email at hello@insightguides.com. Thanks!

CREDITS

Explore Rome
Editor: Sian Marsh
Author: Solveig Steinhardt, Daniel Mosseri
Layout: Aga Bylica
Update Production: Apa Digital
Managing Editor: Carine Tracanelli
Picture Editor: Tom Smyth
Cartography: original cartography Berndston and Berndston, updated by Carte
Photo credits: Alamy 7M, 25, 112, 114, 114/115, 122, 136, 137T; Alessandra Santarelli/Apa Publications 90; Bigstock 96/97, 98; Dreamstime 4BL; Fotolia 94, 94/95, 95L, 99, 100; Getty Images 4/5T, 8/9T, 26/27T; image-BROKER/Shutterstock 91; iStock 4MR, 7MR, 18, 26ML, 26ML, 28/29, 31L, 32, 33, 36, 38/39, 41L, 44, 48/49, 50/51, 53L, 52/53, 58/59, 60, 60/61, 68/69, 72/73, 77L, 92, 92/93, 93L, 96, 97L, 100/101, 101L, 117L, 128/129, 130, 131; Leonardo 104, 104/105, 105L, 106, 106/107, 107L, 108, 109, 110; Ming Tang-Evans/Apa Publications 4ML, 4ML, 4MC, 4MR, 4MC, 6TL, 6MC, 6ML, 6BC, 7T, 7MR, 8ML, 8ML, 8MC, 8MC, 8MR, 8MR, 10, 11, 12, 12/13, 13L, 14/15, 16, 16/17, 17L, 18/19, 19L, 22, 22/23, 23L, 26MC, 26MR, 26MC, 26MR, 28, 29L, 30, 30/31, 34, 34/35, 35L, 37, 40, 40/41, 42, 42/43, 43L, 44/45, 45L, 46, 47L, 46/47, 48, 49L, 50, 51L, 52, 54, 55L, 54/55, 56, 56/57, 57L, 58, 59L, 61L, 62, 63L, 62/63, 64, 64/65, 65L, 66, 66/67, 67L, 68, 69L, 70, 71, 72, 73L, 74, 74/75, 75L, 76, 76/77, 78, 78/79, 79L, 80, 80/81, 81L, 82, 82/83, 83L, 84, 84/85, 85L, 86, 86/87, 87L, 88, 88/89, 102/103T, 102MR, 102ML, 102MC, 102MC, 102ML, 113, 115L, 116/117, 118/119, 120, 121, 124/125, 126, 127, 128, 129L, 132, 133T, 133B, 134, 134/135, 135L; Musacchio & Ianniello 123; Scala Archives 24; Shutterstock 89L, 102MR; Starwood Hotels & Resorts 110/111, 111L; Stefano Politi Markovina/AWL Images 1; Susan Smart/Apa Publications 20, 21, 116, 137B
Cover credits: Susanne Kremer/4Corners Images (main) iStock (bottom)

Printed by CTPS – China

Every effort has been made to provide accurate information in this publication, but changes are inevitable. The publisher cannot be responsible for any resulting loss, inconvenience or injury.

DISTRIBUTION

UK, Ireland and Europe
Apa Publications (UK) Ltd
sales@insightguides.com
United States and Canada
Ingram Publisher Services
ips@ingramcontent.com
Australia and New Zealand
Woodslane
info@woodslane.com.au
Southeast Asia
Apa Publications (Singapore) Pte
singaporeoffice@insightguides.com
Worldwide
Apa Publications (UK) Ltd
sales@insightguides.com

SPECIAL SALES, CONTENT LICENSING AND COPUBLISHING

Insight Guides can be purchased in bulk quantities at discounted prices. We can create special editions, personalised jackets and corporate imprints tailored to your needs. sales@insightguides.com
www.insightguides.biz

INDEX

MAP LEGEND

●	Start of tour
→	Tour & route direction
❶	Recommended sight
❷	Recommended restaurant/café
Ⓜ	Metro station
★	Place of interest
❸	Tourist information
⚊	Statue/monument
✉	Main post office
🚌	Main bus station
⛩	Villa

Park
Important building
Hotel
Transport hub
Shop / market
Pedestrian area
Urban area